Cargoes and Capers

The life and times of a London Docklands man

An autobiographical memoir

By

Johnny Ringwood

Cargoes and Capers
(Explanation)

Cargoes: The Docks, Maritime and Life's Loads

Capers: The many I got up to

© Johnny Ringwood 2017

All rights reserved

This book is an autobiographical memoir. Unless otherwise, noted, the author and publisher make no explicit guarantees as to the accuracy of the information contained in this book, and in some cases the names of people and places have been altered to protect their privacy.

John Ringwood has asserted his right under the Copyright, Designs and Patents Act 1988 to be identified as the author of this book.

No part of this publication may be reproduced, distributed, or transmitted in any form or by any means, without the prior written permission of the author, except in the case of brief quotations embodied in critical reviews and certain other non-commercial uses permitted by copyright law. For permission requests, contact the author.

ISBN-13: 978-1544833552

ISBN-10: 1544833555

Design & formatting by Socciones Editoria Digitale

www.kindle-publishing-service.co.uk

Dedicated to Brenda, my Wife, Mate and Rock.

Acknowledgements

I am indebted to the following persons and their willingness to lend a hand, with photographs, anecdotes and their precious time.

Helen Brown
Jimmy Crouch (Short)
Joanne Ringwood
Andrew Baker

Contents

Preface i
One: Introduction - Early Years 1
Two: The Ringwood's 3
Three: At War with Germany 5
Four: Jersey Road 6
Five: Evacuation 10
Six: Return to Jersey Road 13
Seven: The End of the War 17
Eight: My Dad 20
Nine: Fyfield Residential School 25
Ten: Wrong Side of the Law 27
Eleven: Area on the Mend 30
Twelve: A Distressing Time 31
Thirteen: Peacetime Employment 32
Fourteen: The Call of the Sea 34
Fifteen: Dock Work 51
Sixteen: The Army 55
Seventeen: Brenda 71
Eighteen: Back to reality 73
Nineteen: Our first two sons 74
Twenty: Dark Times 75
Twenty-One: The Manor Road Buildings 77
Twenty-Two: West Ham Power Station 81
Twenty-Three: Into the light 84

Twenty-Four: New Home 91

Twenty-Five: New start.. 92

Twenty-Six: Budding Carpenter 94

Twenty-Seven: Council Officer 97

Twenty-Eight: Almighty slap 101

Twenty-Nine: The Appeal 110

Thirty: Fiftieth Birthday 112

Thirty-One: Back to the Mayflower 115

Thirty-Two: A new start 117

Thirty-Three: Health and Safety 119

Thirty-Four: Sporting Times 127

Thirty-Five: New Pastures 136

Thirty-Six: The Big Step 140

Thirty-Seven: After Dinner Speaker! 144

Thirty-Eight: Nearly lost the Peacock 146

Thirty-Nine: Still Learning.. 148

Forty: Calling it a Day 149

Forty-One: Footlights Beckoned.. 150

Forty-Two: The Dockers' Statue 151

Forty-Three: On the Move Again 2002.. 155

Forty-Four: The Steam Ship Robin.. 157

Forty-Five: Finally.. 159

Preface

The life and times of an East London Docklands man.

This is my story, I am just an ordinary fella, born and bred in the East End of London. Smack, bang next to the Royal Victoria dock in 1936.

I Survived, the bombing and blitz during the war, narrowly escaping being wiped out on a couple of occasions. Any Education that was around at that time was somewhat limited to say the least, being continually interrupted by the Luftwaffe.

Like many youngsters of my generation we lived by our wits, and even at a very young age I learnt the art of 'ducking and diving' and consequently fell afoul of the law.

At the age of sixteen I bid farewell to my family and began a life on the 'ocean wave'. Going to places all over the world, that at that time most people only read about. But that was cut short when I overstayed my leave and was called up to do National Service in the Royal Fusiliers.

Had a few very good jobs after leaving the army but some habits die hard and once again blotted my copy book with the Law, but this time it meant I was to become a guest of Her Majesty for a period of time. But a hard lesson had been learned. For the next few years following my release I worked with some youngsters who had been heading in the same direction, and hopefully to prevent them from having the same outcome as me.

But that's enough of the sad stuff, my cranky sense of humour has always held me in good stead as I hope the reader will gather when reading my effort. Fortunately I have been blessed with a very patient wife Brenda, whom again after reading about my very various exploits I think you will agree.

My eighty one years of life resembles a patchwork quilt, and whilst some of the colours are bright, others are more subdued and some of an even deeper hue, but on the whole it's been a wonderful ride, which I hope with me you will enjoy.

One:
Introduction
Early Years

The area known as Custom House in East London was named after the Custom House building situated just inside the perimeter of the Royal Victoria Dock; the dock finally opened after being manually dug out in 1855. At this time, Custom House also became a place where people lived. Each street was built in a uniform way, mostly two-storey terraces, with each structure having a top and bottom flat, comprising two bedrooms, a kitchen/living room, scullery, and lavatory. Compared to modern day standards they were basic, to say the least, but one good thing in their favour was that they were affordable. The rents reflected the wages that were being earned both in the docks and the surrounding factories.

There was a wonderful community spirit, which was created both at home, at work in the docks and factories, and often cemented in the many pubs that existed. Some of the dockside pubs were known as early morning houses where the dock workers would sink a couple of pints before starting work. However, this sense of community would be sorely tested in just a few years, by Germany….as you the reader will see later.

Hobbies at that time included tending allotments where vegetables were grown, which also helped to boost the household income. Separate allotments were required because the houses had very little space at the rear in which anything could grow. However, these spaces, commonly referred to as 'the yard', could also accommodate pigeon lofts, another popular interest at that time.

Indeed, some very famous racing pigeons were bred in the area around the Royal Docks. The men that kept them had their own drinking clubs, and a common sight on Friday evenings would be these men, assembling with their birds in wicker baskets, ready for the weekend race. The next morning the birds were sent by either rail or road to destinations as far away as Scotland, where they were released. The men would then return to their lofts awaiting the arrival of their birds. Each pigeon would be fitted with a rubber band on its leg, and on arrival home, the time was recorded by removing the band and placing it in a clock. The time was then taken to the pigeon club and logged. The winning time of the racing pigeon was then recorded for future reference and eventually, if the bird's time is the fastest over a set period, the owner would be rewarded with an appropriate trophy. Some of these prize winning birds were sold for very high sums for breeding purposes.

And indeed pigeon racing is not only confined to the working classes. Her Majesty the Queen also is a keen member of this Club.

Another familiar sight in my early years was horse drawn vehicles. It was the main way of distributing goods by road, and those deliveries included coal, milk and vegetables. Collections were also made, for example, by the rag and bone man, whose title comes from an even earlier era. It refers to a bygone period when bones were collected to make glue and in some cases handles for walking sticks. Con our next door neighbour in Jersey Road was one such trader and his cry was: "Any old rags for china".

Nowadays many areas are known as dormitory towns, because most of the inhabitants live at a distance from their jobs, but in general, this was not the case for Custom House and surrounding dock areas. Here, also large families were very common, and this could stretch the limited incoming wages, especially when the children were young. Yet somehow we managed to get by.

Generally, the man of the house was the main wage earner, 'the bread winner', and his wife, usually a 'housewife', had the tasks of looking after the home and children: then, when they came of age they would be expected to help supplement the household income. Remember, this was an age when there was no help in the form of electrical appliances, which we now take for granted. All cooking preparation, laundering of clothes and the cleaning of the home were carried out by hand. To be a housewife and mother in those days was no easy ride.

Two:
The Ringwood's

Both my Mum Winifred, "Win", and Dad John were born in Custom House; mum in Mortlake Road and dad in Whiteman Street. Dad was orphaned at a very early age and spent most of his early life in various orphanages. Mum came from a family of three brothers, Bill, Alec, Ernie, and an older sister Christine, "Chris". My Grandad, who died just before I was born, was named James Ewing. He was of Scots origin whereas my Grandmother Mary came from Ireland. Their birthplaces give an indication of the cosmopolitan makeup of the early Custom House people. Contrary to the norm, both Mum and Dad worked in the West End of London. From the age of fourteen Mum was in domestic service in some very elegant houses, according to her, and Dad, also from fourteen years of age, worked in a number of West End hotels as a trainee cook. I imagine this is where they crossed paths and courted, finally marrying in 1935.

Their first home was in a room sub-let from my Dad's aunt Maud, at 57 Adamson Road, Custom House E16, an East London dock dwelling no more than two hundred yards from the Royal Victoria Dock. It was there at 5-30 pm on Friday the 17th January 1936, that I made my debut, weighing in at six and a half pounds, and by Mum's account, already fighting fit and very noisy.

By 1936 most of the dwellings were showing signs of wear, and the air we breathed was very heavily contaminated by coal fires, especially when they were first lit. Nobody had bells on the front door, so when anyone wanted someone to answer, the door knocker would be rapped once for downstairs and twice for the upper flat. The knocker code finished when the houses were replaced by Tower blocks. A good idea really, since if it had continued using the same criteria for someone living on the twenty third floor, the knocking would have sounded like a drum roll!

We didn't live in Adamson Road long before moving to Kentish Town. We had the top flat in a four storey house with one flat in the basement and three above it. We moved there, because dad left his job in the hotels and had secured a job in Gilbey's Gin factory. My Mum said he often came home from work with a smell on his breath that proved he worked there.

My first real memory at this home was of me standing on the kitchen table in the buff. On the left of me was a tin wash basin filled with barely warm water with which Mum gave me the onceover. I gather this was the normal form of ablution for young family members at that time, because of the lack of bathrooms. Of course, as I grew older the basin progressed to a tin bath, which hung on the wall in the back yard. The use of these tin baths became legendary. Usually the kids had the first go and were able to sit down because they were small. They were followed by the parents which meant a wash down whilst standing. I don't like to imagine the condition of the water when we had all finished. The instructions from mum were always the same: "Make sure you have a wee first before you get in that bath"

I do not remember much about that period, primarily because of my very young age, except that on one Christmas my Dad bought me a red pedal car. It was my job to use my new motor to pick up the Daily Mirror every morning from the nearby corner shop. I guess we lived at that address for about three years, before moving back to Custom House. We lived in a number of different roads there before finally settling in 31 Jersey Road, where we lived from early 1940 to 1952

Three:
At War with Germany

Prime Minister Neville Chamberlain met with Adolph Hitler three times in 1938, and the last time he came back holding a document declaring these talks had achieved 'peace in our time". This proved to be a costly and devastating mistake. In his speech on the 1st September 1939, Chamberlain had explained that Herr Hitler was warned that if he did not give assurance to stop his plans to invade Poland then we would be left with no alternative but to join with France in going to Poland's aid. No such assurance was given, and from his desk in 10 Downing Street, he informed us that 'the nation was now at war with Germany'.

Very shortly after, Dad was conscripted into the Royal Leicestershire Regiment. I remember his badge was that of a tiger, but as soon as the army learnt of his cooking abilities he was transferred into the Catering Corps. I was too young to realise the seriousness of all that was happening, but I do remember missing him and when he finally came home in his uniform, I asked my Mum why he was dressed like that. Mum answered that it was because he was a soldier and along with all his other mates who are dressed the same, it is their job to make sure we are protected against any nasty men who would try and hurt us. Simple, and even my little mind got the gist of what she was saying.

Four:
Jersey Road

Jersey Road is where this story really begins because that is where my memory becomes much clearer. We lived in the bottom flat which, as already stated, consisted of two bedrooms, a kitchen/living room, a scullery and in our situation, because we lived on the ground floor, an outside lavatory. The only heating was from a cast iron range with a very small fire area, which meant in the winter the flat was like a fridge, apart from the area immediately in front of the fire. I clearly remember that women who sat too close to these fires developed a mottled pattern on their shins, which we cruelly called corn beef legs. Money was always tight and one of our neighbours had no doors in their flat because all of them had been removed and used for fire wood. The situation was worsened because of the war with Germany when coal was one of the many things which were rationed. So, we were limited to one hundredweight a week, which meant that the fires could not be lit until late afternoon. In our case that was when we came home from school. At the other end of the day, many of us would go to school very early and sit round the radiators in the cloakrooms to gain a bit of warmth. I was a pretty tough kid but I do remember crying one morning because I was so bitterly cold, and chilblains were a very common ailment.

I'm afraid that because of the lack of hot water, personal hygiene took a bit of a back step. My logic was that you only needed to wash the areas on show, those being the face and hands. But my Mum had realised this and on arriving home from work she would lift up my face and look under my chin for what she called 'tide marks' showing the limit of my ablutions. Then, another of her sayings was "I could grow spuds in those ears".

My brother Jimmy was born in October 1939 and as soon as my Mum decided he was big enough to sleep with me, at about one year old, I bullied him into bed first to warm it up. I remember on one occasion Mum had left for work, leaving me in charge, so it was my job to prepare some breakfast for me and Jimmy. This normally consisted of bread and hot milk, so I put the milk in a pot which I then placed on the gas oven to heat. Because I had other chores to do, I told Jimmy to call me once he saw the milk bubbling, and to enable him to see the milk, I stood him on a chair next to the stove. In a very short while he called out to tell me, but in doing so turned round and knocked the handle of the pot with his leg, Resulting in the contents of the now boiling milk going over the lower parts of his bare legs and feet, causing very quickly large blisters to form. By then Jimmy was screaming in pain, so I ran out into the street shouting for help; neighbours quickly responded and somehow, through their help, an ambulance arrived and took him to Whipp's Cross Hospital in Wanstead. You have to remember this was carried out without present day facilities. For instance, there were no telephones at home, or any other means of communication which we now take for granted.

Mum finally came home, and was in a very distressed state, on seeing me and hearing about what happened, but instead of bawling me out for being so stupid, she gave me a hug and asked me if I was alright. I have never forgotten that act of understanding and motherly kindness. The next day Mum took me to see Jimmy in hospital, but to make me look a bit respectable she bought me a pair of navy blue short trousers, but no underpants. Now the material of these trousers was extremely itchy, and to this day I am not sure who was the more uncomfortable, me or Jim!

I guess when I reflect on the conditions and the limited amount of income, we would be considered pretty poor. During the time Dad was in the army, my Mum who was a very tiny, frail woman, worked in Spillers flour mill, pushing 2cwt of flour around on a wheel barrow. What furniture we had was in a very tatty condition, and because of the lack of heat the flat was very damp, especially in the winter. We had no sheets or pillow cases for the beds and the blankets were also in very short supply: it would always be a bonus when my Dad came home on leave because he would put his big army overcoat on our bed to help counter the terrible cold. We did however, have other creatures to keep us company. The bed bugs that lived behind the peeling and damp wallpaper also felt the cold, so to counter this they would join us in bed during the night. We were also a means of nourishment for them, as the many bites and red blotches on our skin in the morning would indicate.

Of course, the war years were pretty grim for all concerned, but living in the vicinity of the Docks meant that we were in the 'front line'. Before we got our Anderson shelter, during the frequent air raids, my Mum would throw an old mattress over the coals in our coal cupboard which was situated under the stairs leading to the upstairs flat, then the three of us would huddle together until the 'all clear' siren sounded. In later years I would often wonder about my Mum's logic in thinking that these stairs would offer us any kind of protection if a bomb dropped close by. I have one vivid memory of her during one of these raids: she was on her knees in the cupboard, barely visible in the candle light, praying that the bombs we could clearly hear landing would miss us. Thankfully, her prayers were answered.

After a while, an Anderson shelter was erected in our back yard and on hearing the siren, which indicated that we were about to cop it, we would all rush in. On one such occasion my Dad was home on leave, and unfortunately, during the raid, he was caught short and needed to use the outside lavatory. Whilst he was in there, a bomb dropped very close to us causing extensive damage to our house. However, my main concern was for my Dad, so I burst through the shelter door banging on the door of the lavatory shouting out "Dad are you alright?" He staggered out covered in dust and said "No I'm not alright! I pulled the chain and the F*****g house fell down!"

On another occasion my Mum thought it would be safer for us if we were to use the big public shelter in the nearby Becton Road Park. It was night time on this occasion and Mum was carrying Jimmy in her arms. In many areas of the park there were small fires. I learnt later that these were incendiary bombs, which would explode and set light to the roofs of houses when landing. We were in the public shelter one night when a bomb landed very close, and when leaving the next morning we found that it had taken out many houses in Sophia Road. That was the next turning to us in Jersey Road - another near miss.

Before I move on I want to explain that all of the above was the norm to me. I have little or no memory of my first three years of life. Of course, they were hard times but I had no recollection of what might be called good times, so I found it hard to make any kind of comparison.

Much later in life when I was in my sixties, I was teaching first aid to a class of thirty. I asked the class during one period if there were any questions, and out of the blue a young fella said: "I bet you've got a few bob John"? I guess he made this assumption because I had a nice Jaguar car, the clothes I wore were smart and of good quality, and I owned my own home. "Yes", I replied "I am a millionaire". "Are you really, John?" he replied. My response was: "In money terms, no, but in comparing and reflecting on my earlier years, I am more than a millionaire, because when I was a young kid no millionaire at that time appeared to have many of the things that I have now." I left it there, but invited the class to just dwell on the differences between what we had in the forties and what I and they have now. The one thing I am totally thankful for is that when I get up in the morning, in order to warm my home all I have to do is switch on the central heating.

Five:
Evacuation

The blitz was now in full swing and Mum decided that enough was enough, and that evacuation was the next thing for me and Jimmy. Many other mothers from the dockland areas also held this view. So one morning, along with my cousins Jean, Ted and Pat who lived a couple of doors from us at number 27 Jersey road, we were scrubbed up and had labels tied on to indicate who we were. At our departure place in Plaistow we were assembled in groups. I remember all the mums were in tears, mine especially, considering our ages: I was six and Jimmy was nearly three. After a final hug my mum said "Johnny please make sure you are not separated". We then boarded buses and were taken to one of the London mainline stations. Accompanying us were a number of other children from Custom House and the surrounding areas.

In later years I have often seen photographs of other evacuees at these departure points. In most cases they were smartly dressed in school uniforms, each carrying small leather cases, and they looked pretty healthy. I am afraid our group didn't reflect this image at all. Some of us had lost everything during the air raids and had suffered extreme hardships, but our mums, God bless them, sent us off looking as good as they could.

What I remember of the train journey is pretty hazy. However, I do remember that a lot of the children were crying and my cousin Jean suffered badly from travel sickness. With regards to Jimmy and me, I think we were both too young to appreciate the gravity of it all. Our destination was Skipton in Yorkshire and on arriving we were assembled sitting on benches in a church hall. After we had been given food and drink, people started arriving. They walked up and down the rows of benches giving us the once over. They then went to the back of the hall to discuss their choice. Much to my distress and verbal objections, Jimmy was the first one chosen to be taken away by a nice man and woman. He was lifted up by the man and off they went. By now I was in a right old state, and said to one of the people who was looking after us: "But my Mum said we must keep together". She replied "I am really sorry son, but things do not always happen the way we would like them to". So that was it, I felt really guilty that I had let my Mum down.

One by one the children were taken away to their new homes until there was just me. I don't blame anyone for not picking me out, because what with my scrawny build and pale complexion I don't think I would have been my first choice either. Finally, late in the evening two elderly ladies took me home. I must have made a distinct impression because the next morning they brought me back. At last a man arrived and asked me if I would like to live with his family. By this time I had just about had enough and would have gone home with Count Dracula. When we got outside the building, there, waiting on the kerb was his beautiful Wolseley car. Wow! I thought I've cracked it! You see, I had never been in a car before. His house was on the edge of the Moors and looked really nice. We were greeted by his wife and son who was, I guess roughly the same age as me. Straightaway I felt that the wife was not keen on the idea of having this little urchin coming into her household. After a really nice meal and BATH both her son and I, who was named Jimmy, funnily enough, retired for the night to his bedroom.

The next day, at breakfast I started scratching my head. This was observed by the lady of the house with some alarm. She asked why I was doing this, and I replied I might have a few fleas (curtesy of the public air-raid shelter). Then the husband was dispatched straight away to the nearest chemist for a flea comb. On arriving back I was taken outside to the garden area where, on my instructions, a newspaper was stretched over a table and the comb applied to my hair. Sure enough the little blighters started to fall. I was very skilled at dispatching them, which was achieved by cracking them with the back of the thumb nail on to the hard surface of the table. By now the lady was pulling her hair out, and with that, both she and her husband went into the next room to discuss my future. The first thing that happened was that all of my clothes were disposed of and I was taken to the barbers where I had what is now called a number one haircut, or as we called it a 'tupney all off'. My camp bed was then taken out of the son's bedroom and repositioned on the stairs landing.

It did not bode well. I cannot complain about how I was looked after but I was not comfortable with the situation and neither were they. I went to the local school for the very short period I was in the area. There was a little bit of bullying with regards to my cockney accent, but a couple of playground fights soon sorted that out. This all sounds a bit negative, but thinking back on it, I think I can understand where they were coming from. I really didn't fit into their world: they were a nice middle class family who were suddenly confronted with this scruffy, lousy cockney with an attitude, partly because I had the raving hump after being separated from my brother. But it was not all bad. The man of the house had a haulage company, and on occasions he would let me accompany one of his lorry drivers delivering goods etc. Sometimes the driver would take me to his home and his lovely wife would feed me up with delicious grub, which was when I got to appreciate real Yorkshire hospitality.

Okay, it did not work out for me, but it did for many other thousands of evacuees - my three cousins and brother included. The people who accepted these children, many of whom were in traumatised and malnourished condition, must never be forgotten. These wonderful folk not only opened up their homes, but also their hearts. In some cases these loving relationships have lasted right up until the present day.

In due course my Mum came to visit. We had a chat and she could see I was not very happy, and when she saw my sleeping arrangements that capped it. Mum thanked the man and wife for looking after me so well, since I certainly did look a lot better than when I first arrived, and we got ready to go back to the East End.

Six:
Return to Jersey Road

So with final farewells my bag was packed and then Rupert, the man of the house, gave me a wooden writing box (I had often admired the one his son had) and ten shillings, a very touching gesture which I really appreciated.

The family that took in my brother Jimmy looked after him really well for nearly two years and were very refined, so when it was his time to return he came home with a very posh accent which Custom House soon blunted. Because of the constant bombing, Custom House and the surrounding docklands, especially Tidal Basin were in a pretty rough state. Most streets had large gaps where houses had been destroyed, and fatalities were also on the increase. They would have been a lot higher if it had not been for warning sirens and shelters.

On the 23rd April 1941, their Majesties King George V1 and Queen Elizabeth made a visit to Freemasons Road, to witness first-hand how badly the area had been affected. This certainly helped to lift morale, but I also believe the visit chimed with a bomb hitting Buckingham Palace, and her Majesty remarking that 'now I can look the East End in the face'.

One of the worst instances of the blitz was when a local school named South Hallsville was bombed. Many hundreds of people were awaiting evacuation in the main cellar the night it was hit, and it was that part of the building which took the full blast. Officially, 73 were reported dead, but many local people believed it was in the hundreds. Another rumour which circulated was that the people should have been picked up in the evening before the bombing, but it didn't happen because the drivers were given the wrong address, having been directed to Camden town instead of Canning town. But, probably, the truth can now never be verified.

Even as youngsters we could determine by engine noise whether it was an enemy or friendly aircraft flying overhead, which gave us a bit of time to seek shelter. Another regular sight was the large number of barrage balloons that flew in the air over London, and at night time the skies were constantly patterned with search lights looking for approaching enemy aircraft, to enable the anti- aircraft guns a better chance of hitting their target.

Sometime during the war, I am not sure when exactly there was a sudden, massive influx of American servicemen. I remember how smart they looked in comparison to our fellas, especially the lower ranked soldiers in their ill-fitting battle dress. The Americans' uniforms made them look like film stars. This did create some tension, because in many ways our boys found it difficult to compete when it came to the ladies. In addition, they had more money and perhaps a certain charisma attached to being from the USA. There was a well-known saying at that time that they were 'over paid, over sexed and over here'. However, one of the things I did like about them was they seem to have a surplus of chewing gum, and every time you met one of these guys the immortal phrase uttered was: "Got any gum chum?" Another thing that the ladies found attractive was that these guys seemed able to get hold of nylon stockings, a further incentive to forming relationships! However, other women found a cheaper way of giving the impression of wearing stockings, which was achieved by using gravy browning to darken their legs and getting someone to draw a straight line down the back of the leg with a thick pencil.

At that time, the pubs in Custom House proved very popular with these visitors, although they did not like our warm beer. One pub in particular, 'The Steps', in Victoria Dock Road, was used on occasion, by ladies of the night. On one particular evening, at about nine o'clock, me, and three mates were watching one of these ladies outside the pub having a cuddle with an American soldier, which I assumed to be the prelude before the main event. They must have been discussing how much money would be required for her services, when the American, who seemed a little bit the worse for wear, suddenly pulled out a large wad of notes, and we heard him say: "Don't worry honey I'm loaded". To prove the point he fanned a wad of money, but what he didn't notice was that one of the notes fluttered to the floor. He may of not have noticed but I did, and with that, I walked passed the couple, pretended to stumble, picked the note up and stuffed it down my sock. He did not see what I had done, but the girl did. She gave me a little wink, and nod which meant I should exit sharpish, which I did.

Then, I split the note, which turned out to be ten shillings, between the four of us, which meant we had half a crown each. We went into a nearby café and had a feed on meat pies; I would like to say they were delicious but they were not. I am sure that if the origins of the meat could have been determined, there would have been links with the Grand National.

As I am writing this episode about the American and the prostitute, it sounds like something out of a Dickensian novel, with me playing the part of an opportunist thief like the Artful Dodger. Was it wrong? In the cold light of an adult present day, of course it was, but reflecting on what it was like in those days with so much deprivation, maybe the reader can understand a little of why I did it.

Just when we had got somewhat use to standard raids from aircraft, Germany introduced a far more dangerous mode of killing machine in the shape of a V1 rocket or as we got to call it, the doodle bug. But we even got a bit blasé with this beast because you could hear it coming, and from its tail there would be a very visible flame. So, as long as it was flying over it was not a problem, but as soon as the engine stopped, you had to take cover because down it would come. Custom House by now had many bomb sites which we called debris, these were our adventure playgrounds

It was on one these sites, in Freemasons Road where a pub called The Gog had once stood, but had been demolished by one of the above mentioned doodle bugs. On this particular occasion, I was with two brothers named Jimmy and Davy Lee and another kid called Sparrow: I had to leave them because my Mum wanted some errands run. Jersey Road was about five minutes away and just as I was going through the front door there was an almighty blast that blew me up the passage. This time, a V2 rocket had hit the same site and killed my three mates along with twelve other people who were in the area. The date was 13th January 1945. Unlike the doodle bug there was no warning with this V2, a monstrosity weighing 27, 600 lb, 45 feet and eleven inches in length, and travelling faster than the speed of sound.

I think our morale was at its lowest at this point. We had survived the blitz, but we did not seem to have any answers to combat this weapon. I think my near miss really got to my Mum and what with her also being very heavily pregnant, she decided we had to get away and after packing our few belongings we went to stay with friends in Whitstable. Whilst we were there my sister Irene was born on the 23rd February 1945. I remember this period as the most relaxing time of the war: Whitstable was and is still a lovely spot and we stayed there for a few months. As the weather began to warm up Jimmy and I spent most of our time on the beach: in addition, I have a couple of outstanding memories of this time. Firstly, the man in whose house we were staying made little lead soldiers, and secondly because sugar was in short supply, Mum would put syrup in my tea which was bloody horrible! After what seemed a very long time, there were signs that we seemed to be winning the war, so home from Whitstable we came.

Soon after arriving home my Dad returned to us on embarkation leave. The very large tented camp from which this embarkation was to take place was situated in a large area of Tidal Basin which had been flattened by bombs during the blitz. This was handy because Dad was able to come home every night. One night he said to me "Johnny I want you to walk pass the camp at exactly half past ten exactly tomorrow morning". He then described precisely the position of perimeter fence at which I needed to be. The next day I followed his instructions to the letter, and lo and behold a beautiful leather 'T' cut football came sailing over the fence. Now, wasn't that a coincidence! Needless to say, I carried on kicking the ball without pause, as if I had been doing so all along the road.

Seven:
The End of the War

All through the war we were encouraged by Vera Lynn, a very popular singer, known by all as the forces sweetheart. One of her songs was "When they Sound the Last All Clear", and these words encapsulate what we all dearly hoped and wanted to happen. Then, on one glorious day, the 2nd September 1945, 6 years and a day from when the war started, they came true. What followed was weeks of celebrations. I went to one family 'knees up' (party) and I remember all my uncles wearing different uniforms and hats. Except for the celebrations and our boys coming home, things seemed to remain the same, for example, it would be quite a long time before rationing finally ended.

In the years after the war Custom House took a long time to get it together. I have a clear memory of many of the men returning to the docks still wearing remnants of their forces uniforms. These included berets of different colours, leather jerkins as worn by the Tank Corps and the cobble stones would echo to the sound of hob nailed boots. In addition, some men would fix on to their leather belts lots of brass badges of different regiments. But gradually we got back into the swing of things and Dad for one, made the transition from the army to ship repairing in the docks

When I was about ten my dad took me to work and we boarded a boat on which he was employed called the Mooltan. From that very moment I knew that I would follow my three uncles and later my dad, into the Merchant Navy.

Jersey Road Peace Time

In my eyes, Jersey Road was akin to a village. We even had a grocery shop and a tobacconist. The community spirit was very strong, as we had all been through very rough times and had stuck it out together through thick and thin. Many of the families were very large, for example in one there were fourteen children and a mum and dad which meant a tight squeeze in four bedrooms.

Security was such that in many cases, to gain access through the front door, all you had to do was pull on a cord which protruded from the letter box and which was attached the key to the front door. I suppose the logic of this was that we didn't have anything of much value to steal.

Again, unlike today, mums felt safe in leaving their babies in prams outside the front door, and because no one owned a car, the road was our fulltime playground. Also, because we had no distractions, like televisions or computers, I am of the firm belief that we spent more time together as mates, thus forming very strong friendships, and in my case, some of these have lasted a lifetime. Another common feature was the sight of mums standing in groups on their door steps having a good old natter, another bit of history that does not really seem to happen anymore, except perhaps outside school play grounds.

As for the men of the households, like my Dad they were hard working, and liked to sup a few beers especially at the weekend. Now, Custom house is split by two main roads, Freemasons and Prince Regents Lane. Our house was in the Freemasons area in which there were three pubs and, when the Gog was rebuilt, four. For a good night out any one of these four pubs offered great entertainment. All of them had an upright piano, and the soloists performing were home grown, my Dad being one of them. The children were always taken along, but of course not allowed into the drinking area. Instead we would be left in the lobby, which most pubs had, and here we would be nourished with a glass of lemonade and a packet of Smiths crisps. If we were very lucky, we would also get a small plate of cockles smothered in copious amounts of vinegar and pepper, and this remains one of my favourite foods. At that time, the cost was three pence and this treat was purchased from a family friend who ran a cockle stall outside the pub. I use to love these nights out, listening to the music and to the mums and dads having a good time. It was so very different from a few months earlier, when we were cowering in shelters and wondering if we would ever see our dads again.

On the subject of leisure time, nobody ever really went on holiday. The only people who left Jersey Road were those who went to Kent to pick hops. They would take a few belongings, jump on the back of a lorry and off they went. The farmers who grew the hops provided very basic corrugated tin huts to accommodate the pickers, who earned a few bob and came home looking very tanned.

Eight:
My Dad

Finally, thankfully, Dad was home for good. My earlier memory of him was as a soldier in uniform, because I was very young when the war started. Then suddenly he appeared in his demob suit, trilby hat and raincoat. He was almost a stranger. He had changed. The war had taken its toll. He liked his drink and when he had too much he would become very argumentative and on occasions, spiteful to my mum. I used to be in bed listening when they came home from the local pub, hoping the conversation would be of a good nature, but now and again he would have one of his 'strops' on. I used to listen as the words became louder and louder. Although she was very small my Mum was feisty and sometimes would worsen the situation by given him back verbally, as good as she got. Inevitably this would lead to her getting a clump. On hearing her cry out, I would fly out of bed and try to diffuse the situation, but by this time it was too late. I was only a little kid, just over nine years old and it used to knock me sick when it happened.

In later years one of the subjects I studied at Barking College of Further Education, was Behavioural Science, which included dealing with confrontation. I was immediately reminded of my Mum and Dad's differences. This is how it was explained to us. To have a confrontation you needed a trigger, or in my dad's case triggers, which I think were his experience of war and alcohol. Secondly, to worsen the condition you need an accelerator, which is where Mum came in, not standing for his verbal abuse, but coming right back at him. Therefore, the risk factor for escalation is high. So how do you reduce it? There was no easy solution. In dad's case, how can you reduce the effects of the war? You can't, it was too late. Some might say it would have been simple to knock the alcohol on the head but there is a real problem with this logic in view of the prevailing work culture at the time. Dad worked in the docks in a gang of casual ship repairers, which meant that at the start of each job, you would assemble on 'the cobbles' a generic term for areas where casual labour waited to be picked by a charge hand. If you were a regular member of the gang then you would be picked. All the members of these gangs worked together and they drank heavily together, which was almost a requirement. Like it or not, this was part of docklands culture. Fortunately, Dad was later taken on as a regular, because he was seen as a hardworking man at Rye Arc on the Isle of Dogs, so the boozing eased back at bit.

In Mum's case I used to plead with her, to basically just shut up. She always replied that this was easier said than done, because in their arguments, nine times out of ten she was right and he was wrong. Then I would ask if it would not be easier to bite her tongue rather than risk getting another black eye. As I got older and bigger, I had a bit more control in diffusing these situations, which helped a bit, but….

I have included the last chapter in my life's journey to show that that not all war wounds are visible and can have far reaching consequences. On reflection I wonder if dad was suffering from what would now be called post-traumatic stress. Like most service personnel he had never talked about his war time experiences, so we will never fully realise what caused this distressing condition.

Dads Toot Bag

Despite all of this I grew to love my dad. He was a real character. After leaving the army, his job in the docks involved working mostly in the ships' engine rooms but occasionally he would become a scaler which meant that his main task would be to chip off rust from ships hulls. Whilst carrying this work, he would pick up little bits of lead, copper, brass and bronze that were surplus to the job, supposedly. He would then stash them in what he called his toot bag. Normally, he would bring his bounty home on a Sunday morning when it was less busy and not so many watchful eyes about. However just as he was entering Jersey Road, a policeman on a bike saw him and gave chase. Now Dad was a bit lively on his toes and beat the copper. He ran into the bedroom jumped into bed fully clothed, boots an all, and said to Mum: "been here all night girl, RIGHT?"

Now the policeman had seen Dad run into a house, but amongst a row which all looked the same, and he knocked on number 29 which was next door to us. After a lot of banging on the door knocker, old Con our neighbour peered round and asked what he wanted. The policeman replied "I have just seen you run in here with a bag over your shoulder". Con then said: "Run you silly Pratt, I can hardly f******g walk", and with that he waved his badly deformed leg about. The policeman apologised profusely and said it must be next door, so then started banging on our door. My Mum answered it and enquired as to what he wanted. The policeman repeated what he had said to Con. And mum said: "I don't know what you are talking about, my old man's been here all night and you have just woken him up"! The policeman was not happy with that and insisted that he be shown the recently awakened husband. What happened next was that he was shown into the bedroom, where my Dad was seen lying in bed with the bed clothes tightly tucked under his chin, giving an Oscar winning performance of someone who had been rudely awaken from his slumbers. With that the policeman said: "Sorry mate", and gave up, having given it his best shot.

One over the eight (or bollard)

London was prone to heavy fogs, due primarily to the thousands of coal burning fires, and on one particular foggy night, Dad arrived home soaking wet. He explained he had been cycling along the dock edge, when he hit one of the large dockside bollards, he exclaimed "I went over the bleeding handle bars straight into the dock". Now in most cases that would have been it, because the chances of getting out again would have been virtually zero. But his guardian angel must have been right on his shoulder that night, because at the exact spot where he went in there was a ladder fixed onto the side of the dock wall. These ladders were very few and far between. In addition, because it was winter the water temperature would have been very low and combined with his intoxicated condition it would have led to his succumbing very quickly to the cold. At that time the unwritten rule was that if you fell into the dock, you were sent to hospital and quarantined for twenty four hours because the water of the dock was so polluted. Mum reminded him of this, but he replied: "Sod that, I'll get done for being drunk and incapable", and with that he went into the scullery and had a wash down.

Mum pronounced that the clothes stank and that she would not be washing them, so all except his boots went on their merry way into the dustbin. On his return from the scullery he looked at me and I shook my head and burst out laughing. In no time, mum joined me. Of course it was serious, but it could only happen to him, especially when he said: "To top it all, I've lost me bleeding cap". Mum replied: "That's not all you have lost, take a look in the dustbin".

Dad the Decorator?

Our flat in 31 Jersey Road at the end of the War was in a very dilapidated condition, so Dad decided to decorate our kitchen/living room. The first thing he said had to go was the gas light fixed into the wall over the metal fire range. The gas to the mantle was via a copper tube and Dad started to yank the tube backwards and forwards until it broke. He obviously thought the gas supply had been isolated when electricity had been fitted, but unfortunately it hadn't, and the gas started jetting into the room. What must be remembered is that unlike today's gas supply, this was fuelled by coal which was extremely toxic and highly inflammable. I cried out: "Bloody hell Dad, what have you done?" He said: "Don't worry boy, there's only a shilling in the meter so it will it will soon run out, but in the meantime get me that old length of rubber tube". This I did. He then fixed the tube over the gas outlet and ran it out into the back yard. Suddenly there was a mighty hollering from our neighbour Con, who shouted: "John what the hell are you doing? All my f*****g chickens are falling over". Dad replied: "Sorry Con, but for gawd sake don't light a fag or they will be roast f*****g chickens". He then lit the gas ring on the cooker to burn off the remaining gas, whilst at the same time squeezing the tube together with a pair of pliers. Then he said: "That's it sorted". But when Mum came home she said: "I can smell gas, John". "Nah, he replied it's your imagination". She said: Well I ain't going to argue with you", and with that she contacted the landlord who owned the flat, and told him that the mantle had been damaged during the bombing. It was now leaking gas, and although a temporary repair had been attempted, it needed fixing. The landlord responded by sending a man round to effectively seal it off.

On another night he came home carrying a large tin. On entering the kitchen he said to mum: "Had a result today gal, got a lovely tin of brown paint really cheap, just the job for the front passage". Mum raised her eyebrows with a look of resignation which said, here we go again. So the weekend came, and Dad had no work that day, so armed with his little paintbrush, set about applying his artistic skills to the walls of the passage. The area he was addressing was the lower half, which was made up of three inch tongue and grooved wood. By late afternoon he was finished and except for a few runs it wasn't bad. I was standing nearby and turning to me he said: "What do you think boy". I replied: "Smashing Dad, you've done a great job". Next morning on my way out to do my paper round, I touched the paint and it was still wet, I called out to Dad "paint's still wet Dad". He replied: "That's all right boy, good paint always takes a time to dry".

Well, it never did completely dry, and over the years along with a few flies and spiders that had stuck to it, developed a rather lovely fluffy condition. I think he invented flock wall paper with an inbuilt collage. Mum and Dad used to love having parties and our guests could always prove attendance, because they invariably left curtesy of Dad's passage with a little smudge of his work of art on their clothing.

Dad also liked to hang wallpaper and almost every year he would give our kitchen/living room the once over. There were two problems with this practice. He never removed the old wallpaper, preferring to leave it on, because as he would say 'it's good insulation', which in turn seemed to make an already small room look even smaller year by year. Secondly, he never moved the sideboard to decorate behind it, his logic being that no-one is going to look behind the furniture. When we finally moved I swear it came out like a cork out of a bottle, leaving a fairly big hole, God knows what the new tenants thought when they moved in.

Dad died at a comparatively young age of sixty eight, with lung cancer, caused according to the doctors, by smoking rolled up Old Holborn cigarettes from a very young age. Mum and Dad's home after Jersey Road was thirteen floors up in a Tower Block called Settle Point in Plaistow. Dad spent his final months there before being transferred to Samson Street hospital. I used to visit him regularly in Settle Point. On one occasion when I rang the bell, Mum looked through the peep hole in the door and called out to dad: "its Johnny". Dad replied: "Hang on a minute before you let him in". After a short while, the door opened and in I went. I entered Dad's bedroom, and he was lying in bed with an oxygen mask on his face. I had already noticed the cigarette smoke, and said to him: "Dad if you don't put that bleeding cigarette out (which he had concealed under the bed clothes) you are either going to blow us up or burn the flat down. Oxygen and a lit cigarette could be a pretty combustible combination. A rebel till the end, Bless him.

Nine:
Fyfield Residential School

One day just after I turned nine, I caught Mum looking at me with a sad expression on her face. "What's the matter Mum"? I asked. She replied: "Johnny you are so thin and you don't look at all well". The next day she took me to the doctors. He gave me the once over and said that I was very malnourished and looked anaemic. He then gave Mum a letter recommending that I be sent to Fyfield Residential School, for malnourished and generally unwell kids. This was near Ongar in Essex and was run by the old West Ham Council. The powers to be agreed and off I went. I spent seven months there and put on a stone, which I have been trying to get rid of ever since!

On arrival we were met by the Matron who gave me a thorough examination. On completion of this I was issued with the following: one grey collared jumper, one grey shirt, one vest and pair of underpants, one pair of socks, one pair of shoes and a top coat. I was then taken and introduced to children in my age group.

Fyfield was okay. The beds were the same as you would find in a hospital, the linen was changed every week, we had to make our beds every morning and the top blanket was blood red. This is where I learnt how to fold hospital corners. The dormitories were warm and dry, the food was basic but not bad, and coming from my background it was like a five star hotel. After lunch, each day there was a very strange ritual. In a very large hall, at one o'clock precisely, everybody was told to lie on a camp bed, on their right hand side, with arms folded. Nobody was allowed to move. To ensure you did not fidget, two nurses sitting on high stools barked at anyone who moved. At half past one the school bell would sound, indicating that we should repeat the procedure on our left hand side. I believe the logic of this exercise was to enable us to relax and let the lunch digest more easily. As far as I was concerned, it had exactly the opposite effect. I have never felt so tense and uncomfortable in my life and that midway, half hour bell was the longest time spell I have ever experienced.

But God bless them, they must have been doing something right, because in a very short period, I began to fatten up and look a lot healthier. When um and Dad made a visit, after a couple of months of my being there, they could not believe the difference. Another thing I will always thank the school for is giving me a six foot by three foot garden area all of my own, in which I planted some nasturtium seeds. When they bloomed, it gave me a wonderful sense of satisfaction. That introduction to gardening still benefits me today, and I believe that the end products of tending a garden are amongst the best rewards ever.

I remember one morning, when mail from home was being handed out, one of my mates received a parcel in which there were two bananas. I could just about remember them from before the War. I asked if I could have bit and understandably, he refused. Then I asked if I could have one of the skins. He agreed and gave me one, so I spent the next five minutes scraping the inside of this then exotic fruit, with my two front teeth. Even today, some seventy odd years later, I am reminded of this instance, whenever I eat a banana.

Our dormitories were named after local rivers, and I was in the Lea room. One night, just after seven pm, which was the time we were sent to bed, a couple of the boys at my end of the room had a bit of a rumble. The head boy, who was about fourteen came bounding down, and thinking that I was involved gave me a smack around the ear. As I was nearly asleep when it happened it was a bit of a shock and on realising his mistake he apologised. To make up for it took me down to the prefects' room for cocoa and a currant bun. But what I really remember was that there was a radio playing, which was something I had really missed since my stay at Fyfield. I vowed then, that this was something I would never be without again, and I never have.

Ten:
Wrong Side of the Law

I left Rosetta Primary School, and went to Shipman Road senior school at the age of eleven. It was a very old building and the teaching and pupil materials were basic to say the least. Our desks were wooden and had fixed seats that accommodated two of us. The pens were a tube of wood with metal nib fitted, and each desk had two inkwells. One day one of the kids came to school with a Biro ballpoint pen, which I fell in love with straight away. At playtime I mentioned this to one of my mates. He said that he knew a shop up the Abbey Arms where they had a load of them. I said: "Fat lot of good that will do me: where do I get the money to buy one?" "Who's talking about buying one", he replied. Then, with realisation dawning, I asked: "What do you mean, are you talking about pinching one?" He replied: "Not one, but a lot". He went onto explain that they were in the front of the shop window, and to my request for more details he replied that a quick brick through the window would result in them belonging to us. Well, that was it. We were joined by another one of our mates called Bert, and one night at about eleven o'clock we arrived at the scene and did the business. I put both hands through the hole in the window, scooped up a fair amount of Biro ballpoint pens and legged it up the road. Then, finding a quiet spot, I shared the pens between the three of us.

Just as I was entering Jersey Road, I heard a car coming up behind me. Suddenly I heard a voice I recognised as belonging to Bert, saying: "he is the other one who was with me". It appears that Bert, who was not the sharpest knife in the drawer, decided that his share of the pens was not enough, so went back to the scene of the crime to get some more. By now the police were there in the shop talking to the owner, and on coming out, they found dear Bert, with his hands inside the window. With that they chucked him into the back of their car. On their way to Jersey Road they had come across my other mate who was involved, so now they had the three of us. We were taken to Abbey Arms police station, and the three of us were charged with theft. Our parents, who had no idea what we had been up to, were sent for, and a few weeks later we appeared at Stratford Magistrates' Juvenile Court.

By this time, I had had the opportunity to reflect on the stupidity and seriousness of what we had done. I feared that I would be sent to an approved school, all of which had fearsome reputations. I had seen what went on at close quarters, when visiting another one of my Jersey Road mates who was an inmate. So when the day finally arrived for me to attend court and I was standing waiting for my Mum and Dad in our fluffy, painted front passage, gone was the cocky little fella before the robbery, and in his place was one very worried young boy.

Part of the proceedings in the courtroom, involved the parents being asked if they would like to tell the court about the character of their child. My Dad said that normally, I was a decent well behaved boy, and he had no idea that I would be capable of doing something of this nature. The father of my other mate said something similar about his son. But when it came to Bert's Dad's turn, he walked up to the Magistrates desk, on which he casually leaned, and said to the Magistrate: "I want to tell you a little story". He continued: "Me and young Bert went up to Club Row and bought a dozen chicks, brought them home, shared them out, six each and the boy put his in a box ,wrapped them up and put them near the fire. I didn't bother too much with mine and after three days mine were all brown bread (dead), but Bert's were lovely, fat and fluffy, and you wanna see them now strutting and clucking round the yard and all laying eggs". To illustrate the point he did a very good demonstration of a chicken doing exactly that. By now, both I and the rest of the people in attendance, including the Court Clerk, were biting their lower lips to contain the laughter that was bubbling up. But one look from my Mum said 'don't you dare'! The Magistrate, with an alarmed look on his face, peered over his half-moon glasses and said, after clearing his throat: "Oh yes, thank you, thank you for that graphic explanation and testimony".

However, the humour soon stopped when the Magistrate gave it to us big time. He called the three of us to the front of his desk and then laid it on the line saying that if we ever steered off course just one inch, then it would be off to Borstal for up to three years. The final outcome was that we each received two years' probation. With that threat hanging over us, we complied, to the letter.

What struck me as being very strange was that when the Magistrate listed what we had supposedly removed from that very small hole in the window, it included many quite large toys. Well, there you go, that's life. Evidently, someone had a good Christmas! The most ironic thing is that the ball point pens we valued so highly in those days, come for free at least once a week, through charity appeal letters I receive through my letterbox.

Eleven:
Area on the Mend

I had a paper round, which covered a very large area of Custom House and the adjacent Tidal Basin, for over four years, from the age of eleven to fifteen. During that time these areas experienced a revival and I watched them being developed from bombed wastelands into places with well-built houses and flats, which became the Kier Hardie Estate. However, prior to this happening, on many of the spaces as a supposedly 'temporary' measure, American designed, prefabricated, single story buildings were erected, which proved very popular as they had many modern design features. Apparently, 'temporary' was reckoned to be a maximum of ten years, but some of these lasted well over thirty. Later on, one of the better, brick built houses at twenty five Murray Square, became home to myself and my wife Brenda and sons Terry, Steve and Michael, for thirty two wonderful years.

What was good about this development was that the old community spirit that had existed before the war soon returned, but then, with the development of tower blocks this spirit diminished considerably.

Twelve: A Distressing Time

As already stated, Mum was a tiny, frail lady, and even as a child I had noticed that she seemed to be getting smaller. At night, her wracking cough would keep us all awake and Dad finally convinced her that she needed to go to the doctor. When, finally, Mum decided to see her GP, he considered her symptoms to be serious enough to warrant an immediate referral to the hospital for checks. It appears that the deprivations of the war, the damp cold flat, and her smoking had finally caught up with her, and Mum was diagnosed with tuberculous. The X-rays revealed that both lungs were affected, and this was explained to Dad. So the prognosis was not good. If the disease was only in one lung, then normally, it would be removed, but in Mum's case, clearly that did not apply. However, it appears (and this is where my memory is a bit hazy) that a new drug had been discovered, and my mum was one of the first people in the world to be treated with it. Her treatment was provided at a Sanatorium named Marillac, in Warley near Brentwood, run by nuns. Mum stayed for quite a long period. At that time there was some success in treating TB in Switzerland, because of the cold dry air. So it was decided to create, as far as is possible, similar conditions at Marralac. To that end, the patients were placed in beds totally wrapped up and warm, but were on a balcony with the windows open, even in winter, except when it rained. This may have been of benefit for the patients, but it was bloody freezing for the visitors!

It took nearly four years from Mum's first diagnosis to her being given the all clear. Mum, this feisty little lady, finally passed at the age of seventy eight, much loved and missed.

Thirteen:
Peacetime Employment

I left Shipman Road School at the age of fifteen, I think it is fair to say, without too much distinction. Work had started to be more plentiful so most people were employed. Of course, we had the docks and in adjacent Silvertown there were a good number of manufacturing and food processing factories. One of the main employers was Tate and Lyle the sugar refiners. I had a job there prior to going to sea, and my job was to sweep up any spilt sugar from the machines that bagged up the sugar into two pound packs. The machines were operated by women and there were a lot of them. Individually, they were fine but collectively they were always cooking up something, normally at my expense. I was very young at the time and not very worldly regarding the opposite sex, and boy did they know it. To say I blushed a lot is to put it mildly.

The floor on which we worked had a great atmosphere, there was constant music from the ceiling mounted speakers, consisting of songs from the latest hit parade and I always enjoyed hearing the women singing along. Every year the company would have a sports day, when a beauty contest would also be held. There was never any shortage of good looking girls to taking part. Each year they would try and get a celebrity to do the judging, and on this particular occasion it was Dennis Price, who was well known film star. I'm not sure he was the right man for the job because he seemed to spend more time giving us fellas the once over.

I progressed from that part of the factory to the transport section and became a lorry driver's mate. We carried six tons of sugar - four hundred and eighty twenty eight pound packets. There was a competition between the drivers and their mates as to who could unload the six tons in the quickest time, by hand. Bill my driver said "Johnny we are going to win that", and after a lot of practice we did. We managed to unload the lorry in just under ten minutes, and I don't think that record has ever been beaten.

Fourteen:
The Call of the Sea

I mentioned earlier, that prior to marrying my Mum, Dad had worked as chef in a number of high class hotels in London, and after discharge from the army, had a spell of working in the docks. When he had had enough that, he decided to get back to his roots as a cook, but on Merchant Navy vessels. As soon the Shipping Federation saw his references from the hotels they granted his Seaman's Log Book straight away, with chief cook rating.

Before he sailed on his first trip he took me on board and showed me his cabin and the galley. Then he said: "While you're here, you might as well peel some spuds". So I did. I think I was about eleven at the time, and whilst I was getting stuck into the spuds I heard one of the crew say: "Cor blimey, they must be getting hard up, they are recruiting kids". But as soon as I had climbed that gangway, I knew that was where I wanted to be. I had a number of jobs after leaving school at fifteen, but they were just stop gaps. It confirmed my wish to follow Dad and uncles Bill, Ernie and Alec who had been engine room stokers, for a life on the briny.

So the day finally arrived when I had reached sixteen, which was the minimum age for entry to the Merchant Navy. But coming of age was just the first step and a couple of my mates who were already serving, gave me the necessary information on how to proceed. This is how it went: the next stage was attending an interview at the Lloyds Shipping building, in Leadenhall Street, London. The first hurdle was to get past a man at the main entrance. His role was to determine whether you had prepared yourself adequately for the interview; namely were you clean and smart, and he took no prisoners. I knew a couple of fellas who been turned away on such grounds. However, being forewarned I achieved the pass, and reckon I cut the mustard by borrowing my Dad's dark blue raincoat, and wearing a white shirt, dark tie and trousers and making sure my shoes were polished. The actual interview went well, especially when I told them of my family involvement in the Service. Then when they asked in which area I would like to serve, my choice was catering, to which they agreed.

The next step was being sent to Gravesend Sea Training School for eight weeks. It was residential, and not an easy ride, because there was always a long waiting list of people wanting to join the M.N. They expected a very high level of response to the training given, and you did not need to fall far from the required standard to get your marching orders. It was run almost like an approved school for offenders; discipline was very strict and the accommodation was based on the style of two berth cabins. We were taught the rudiments of catering, which included waiting on tables, and various forms of stewarding that would be needed both on cargo and passenger boats. Coupled with that were the basic requirements of cooking and preparation of foods. I learned two valuable lessons whilst I was there. The first happened when one of the instructors was finding it difficult to reach and lift a very heavy object. One of the trainees stepped straight in and gave him a hand. Immediately I thought that that should have been me. If you want to get on, don't wait to be asked. If you see someone struggling with anything, jump in and give them a hand. That attitude has stood me in good stead, not only in regard to my working life, but in life in general. The second time was when I was washing up at the sink after a meal in the house of the Captain who was in charge of the training centre. On finishing washing up the crockery, I then washed down all the working surfaces. On seeing me do this the Captain's wife, said: "I'm impressed. Nobody has done that before". She informed the Captain of what I had done and he looked at me and said: "Well done". This suggested to me that 'going the extra mile' can sometimes pay dividends.

Of course, we were also taught basic seamanship, and encouraged to bear in mind homilies such as the lack of back doors on a ship, and the need, therefore, to ensure that you are well acquainted with lifeboat drills, should everything go belly up. Fortunately, after eight weeks I got through the training. On completion you were given a navy blue jacket and trousers, and on each shoulder was sewn an emblem reading Merchant Navy. On the train coming home, boy was I proud to have this displayed. I felt that I had fulfilled a long held dream.

By now I had been issued with my standard Seaman's Log Book which was to record all the names of the boats on which I was to sail. Other information stated whether the trip was home trade, which meant coastal waters or the continent of Europe, or foreign which included anywhere else in the world. After a very short leave, I was sent a letter telling me to attend the Shipping Federation in the King George V Dock. The man behind the desk said: "Welcome son", and shook my hand. He explained that the first trip would be home trade, that the name of the boat was the Good Hope Castle, of the Union Castle Line, and that I would be joining her as a galley boy. I learned that she would be calling at Rotterdam, Antwerp and Hamburg, that the trip would last about a month, and that I would join her tomorrow. So along with Dad who was home on leave I went into the Royal Albert Dock where she was berthed the next day and boarded her.

I found the galley and the chief cook and introduced myself and my Dad, who told him that he too was a chief cook. As Dad was leaving, he said to my new boss: "Do me a favour mate, keep your eye on him, it's his first trip". But he replied: "Sorry pal, I will be too f*****g busy, to wet nurse him. He will have to look after himself". Dad looked at me, gave a small shrug and said: "Sorry son, welcome to the real world".

The next morning we sailed. The Good Hope Castle was top heavy and wow, did she roll and boy was I seasick. All I wanted to do was to go to my cabin, lay on my bunk and die, but the cook wasn't having any of that. He pointed at the ceiling and said: "That's called a deck head, the walls are called bulkheads, and the floor is called the deck. Now, get a bucket of hot water, a block of that heavy yellow soap and a scrubbing brush and start cleaning them". You horrible git I thought and got really mad, but I had a go. But almost every five minutes I was running to the ship's rail, bending over and 'feeding the fish'. However, a few hours later I began to feel a bit better. I don't know whether my rage took my mind off the motion of the ship, but whatever it was, I was never seasick again.

There were three of us in the one cabin: one steward, me and another boy rating. I was on the bottom bunk below the steward, and just as we were stripping off to get some sleep, the steward leaned over and gave me some of the most important advice I have ever had. He said: "I am sorry mate, but I've got to tell you this, you are really chucking up." "What do you mean? I said. He replied: "Have you ever heard of body odour? I said that I had not. He then explained that everybody sweats and that if you don't get rid of that sweat by daily showering, then you start to smell. He said: "Johnny boy, that's where you are at the moment. Also, you need to wash and change your underwear daily". This advice was really appropriate, especially when the boat you were on went to tropical areas. I can say, honestly, that before this conversation I was not aware there was a problem. But as soon as it was explained it became crystal clear and I have stuck to that regime, except for one spell (which will be detailed later), all of my life.

Ben was the name of the man who reminded me about personal hygiene. He also had a wind up gramophone player and a good selection of jazz and swing records. One of these by a blind pianist, called George Shearing, was a haunting melody called 'You are too Beautiful', and it gave me my first and lasting love of Jazz.

We arrived at Rotterdam, and just as I and the other boy rating were starting to go down the gangway, a young cadet officer gave me the once over, saying with a sneer on his face: "That suit you're wearing (which had been one of my Dad's) is a bit big for you isn't it? Also, you do not wear black shoes with a brown suit". Of course, he was right and I was really embarrassed to have these things pointed out to me. Before I had sailed my Dad said: "Listen Johnny, I've got some words of advice for you. Firstly, listen and learn, and sometimes even when you are right, hold your tongue". Because he knew that I had a bit of an edge to my temper he told me to learn to sit on my fists. Basically, he advised just being a nice fella, so that I would fit into the crew more easily.

So here I was, on my first trip having to try to put my Dad's advice into practice. I gave the cadet a long look, and quietly said through gritted teeth: "Yeah you're right mate", and carried on walking down the gangway, fuming. I vowed that in the future, nobody will ever criticise the way I dress. So from then onwards, after nearly every trip, I would buy a new rig out which always included a bespoke tailored suit. On one occasion I had a Crombie overcoat made at Max Cohen's in Aldgate. It was so well tailored and recognisable, that on one occasion, in Auckland, New Zealand, I was standing outside a shop, waiting for a girlfriend to turn up, when I was approached by a man who was English but lived there, and he said: "Excuse me mate that's a Maxi Cohen coat isn't it?" I replied that he was right. He then he offered to buy it off me, whatever the cost. "Name your price", he said. He was gutted when I answered "Sorry pal, it's not for sale".

I sailed on a good number of ships and for the first three years travelled all over the world. One of these trips was to Canada and the west coast of

America. The ship was named the Vancouver Star and belonged to the Blue Star line. Once again, I was the galley boy, and did not hit it off with the chief cook. No matter how hard I tried he always managed to find fault. However, the second cook and baker was Davie, who was a big man and a lovely fella.

One of our ports of call was New Westminster, which was near Vancouver. The local radio station had a programme called Gangway and because I was the youngest crew member they asked the Skipper if I could do an interview. He agreed and they came aboard, to do it. I was then contacted via the ship's phone by a couple who had heard the programme, and found out where I came from. They wanted to make contact because they had emigrated from Stratford, which was only a couple of miles from Custom House. They took me home and gave me a really great reception, which included lovely grub and a tour of the city. It was a really nice occasion and we parted on really good terms.

Back on board, we sailed from New Westminster to Port Albernie and loaded up with a deck cargo of timber which once again caused the boat to rock and roll. So, on leaving Canada, Davie became ill, and because he was my mate I looked after him until we reached Seattle in America. By then he was very ill and on arriving was taken ashore. Before he left I said "You'll be alright Dave, with lovely nurses to look after you". He looked at me but there was no smile or response, so I knew it was serious. Later on in the day, as I was entering the ship's salon where the officers ate their meals, one of the stewards said "Johnny, have you heard the news about Davie?" I shook my head indicating no. "Sorry mate" he said. "He has died". When he said it I was looking into a mirror and saw from my reflection that my face had turned a deathly pallor. "What did he die of? I asked. He replied "It was polio". Now, for as long as I can remember, the one disease that I had always been frightened of was polio, and knew how contagious it could be. So, as far as I was concerned, because of the close contact I had had with David over the last three days, I had got it.

Our next destination was San Francisco, and we sailed the following day. I was expected to step into the breach and share the work in the absence of David, but I was in bits. My first job in this new role was to chop vegetables into small pieces for a soup, this was done with a large carving knife. The cook looked at me and said: "So he's gone and you are going to have to get over it, and quickly". I did not respond, so he said "Did you hear what I said?" I replied: "Yes". Then he said: "Well make sure you have. I don't want any more of you moping around and you can keep your stroppy attitude under wraps. Do you understand?" I replied: "I do, but do me and yourself a favour chef and just shut up". But he didn't, he just kept on and on. In the end I flipped and threw the knife at him. It just missed him and went out through the porthole. With that he ran out of the galley screaming "The galley boy's gone mad and is trying to kill me". Two of the deckhands who were nearby came in and found me in a very distressed condition. The chief steward was summoned to the scene and said: "You had better go to your cabin and stay there until this can be sorted out".

After about thirty minutes he came back and said: "I have got to take you to the Captain, son". "I understand", I replied. "Let's go". On arriving, we found the chief cook waiting outside. The chief steward knocked on the door and the captain asked him to send me in alone. I entered and he said: "Sit down son and tell me your side of the story". I did so, telling him that because of my close proximity to David whist he was sick and because Polio was so contagious, I was convinced I had contracted it. Then I had to tell him about the conversation that led me to throw the knife. He said in a very soft voice: "Son, I can understand where you are coming from, but you could have killed him". Then, to my surprise he poured out a glass of whisky and said: "Here you are son, get this down you". Then he told me not to worry and that he would be sending me to hospital for a few checks. But in the meantime, (and this is for the two listening outside), in a very loud voice, he said: "Listen to me young man. What you have done was extremely dangerous and I will not tolerate this kind of behaviour, but because I understand the reasons for your stressed condition and because of your unstinting care for the second cook during the illness, I am prepared to let the matter rest. Now, go about your duty and behave yourself. Do you understand?" I replied: "Yes sir, I am sorry". Then he added: "Don't just say sorry to me, but to the chief cook as well." This I did, very unwillingly. Fortunately, I got the all clear from the hospital, but boy was I glad to get off that boat when we docked at Liverpool.

When you sign on a ship bound for foreign countries, the actual contract could be for two years, but normally, that is not the case. Most shipping companies have set journeys, to particular parts of the globe. For instance, the Union Castle Line covered South and East Africa and took nine weeks to complete; the Highland boats of the Royal Mail line journeyed to South America and also took nine weeks; whilst Shaw Saville boats went to Australia and New Zealand and their trips lasted four months.

However, the next boat I sailed on was a very small cargo boat weighing only about seven thousand tons. Her name was the MV Trevose, and she was owned by the Hains Shipping company .We knew that our main ports of call were to be in the middle and far east but once the listed ports of call had been dealt with, she could be called to other ones in these areas to pick up and dispatch other cargoes, thus lengthening the time of the voyage.

The unflattering name used for a boat of this nature was a tramp and the unpredictable time to be spent at sea on such a vessel meant that the two year articles that you initially signed could become a reality. However, on this occasion the trip only lasted seven months. The ports of destination that we did know about included Penang, Singapore, Port Swettenham, Kure and Kobe in Japan. Kure was the embarkation port for the English forces fighting in Korea and Kobe was the port for the American forces. At the age of nearly seventeen these foreign sounding names had a magical and mystical appeal. The world then was very large and it took weeks by boat to arrive at them. Hardly anybody flew. Most passengers travelled by sea as the norm. But now the world seems much smaller, and with the introduction of cheaper air flights, nearly everybody you speak to has had foreign holidays covering most parts of the world. Nevertheless, then as now, and in anticipation of the future I prefer the idea of a much larger world.

The year was nineteen fifty two, and the Korean War was in full swing, we called at Kure because much of our cargo consisted of military supplies. I liked Kure. The girls were beautiful; the Saki, was plentiful and the British forces personnel were great company and bent on having a good time. Many of them were waiting to go to Korea for the first time, whilst others were on leave from there. The Korean War is often called the forgotten one, and this should never be the case. When speaking to these fellas, then and more recently, they always say how tough it was, and that the enemy was as fanatical as any present day foe in this divided world.

Our next port of call was Kobe: this was the American main embarkation port for Korea. I decided that the more I saw of Japan the more I liked it. On leaving there, I asked one of the deck officers where our next port of call was. The officer replied that he could not answer that yet, and that I would be told once we reached the open sea. Once clear of the harbour, we were informed that our next port would be Takuba in China. On querying all the secrecy, we were told that that is how the Chinese wanted it. The next set of rules that had to be complied with was the handing in of all cameras held by any member of the crew. They had to be kept in bond and on arrival the bond would be locked and remain out of bounds. Also, this meant that any cigarettes or alcohol would be denied until we left. The other more worrying aspect was that the wireless room would be locked and out of action until we sailed, which meant we would be completely isolated from the outside world.

A few days later the Chinese coast line came into view and when it seemed that we were still a few miles off, the engines stopped and the anchor was lowered. An hour or so later we sighted a tug pulling some barges and approaching us. On their arrival our gangway was lowered down the side of the ship. The personnel that came on board included a Chinese official, two Russians, a Swiss interpreter and six soldiers armed with rifles. With a red star prominently displayed on their hats, their uniform was the padded type, exactly similar to that of the communist enemy our boys were fighting in Korea. It all seemed very strange. Although it was known at that time that China liked to play things close to their chest, all this appeared divorced from reality, and the crew was very uncomfortable with the whole situation. After a few days, some of our cargo was loaded onto the barges, and when that was completed we took on board some assorted cargo from them. Finally to every ones' relief we pulled up the anchor and sailed away. I did not enjoy the uncertainty of that episode one little bit.

Just as we were leaving the Chinese coast we met a force twelve typhoon. I have already mentioned the size of our craft, which meant we were bounced around like a cork. Also, one of the most terrifying movements of the ship in these kinds of conditions was called a corkscrew, when the bow of the ship ploughed deep into the ocean causing the stern to lift and the propellers to race. At the same time she would roll from side to side, so that at its most extreme, the hand rail seemed almost level with the sea. I remember vividly that on one occasion, the boat rolled deeply over to starboard, juddered and then seemed to just stay there. I am sure all of the crew thought, at that moment, this is it, but then thankfully she just managed pull out of it. The captain gave the order that nobody should sleep or go on deck and that everyone must wear their lifejacket, until the storm abated. If the order had come that we had to abandon the ship and board the lifeboats, there was no way we could have lowered them. I have certainly seen the sea in its most extreme moods, one as described above and also when it is as flat as a millpond.

Bum Boats

Aden in the Red Sea and Port Said at the entrance to the Suez Canal (when coming from the UK) were both refuelling ports, so the crew hardly ever got ashore. To counter this, local tradesmen would bring their wares up to our anchored ships by rowing boat. These were known by all and sundry as Bum Boats. Sometimes money would change hands, mainly from passengers on the Liners and on one occasion, one of the items for sale was a beautiful yellow leather suitcase. Whilst standing at the ship's rail looking down at this near work of art, I was approached by a very well-spoken female passenger who had obviously taken a shine to it. She asked "how would one go about purchasing it?" Having dealt with these guys on a number of former occasions, I replied: "This is how it goes. You ask him how much for the suitcase. He will reply, something like, 'you speak lady you tell me how much you think', then you offer him a low price and it goes on from there". So, as instructed the transaction proceeds.

The passenger	"How much for that yellow suit case"?
The boat man.	"You speak lady, how much you think"?
The lady in her wonderful refined accent	"Fave shillings"
The boat man	"You f******g crazy lady?".

The passenger then said to me. "Was that offer a tad low steward"? "Maybe just a trifle madam", I replied. I looked down at the man who was pointing to the lady with one hand and the index finger on the other hand was moving in a circular motion around his temple.

The next incident was in Aden. I had been had over a number of times, by a bum boat man who liked to be called McGregor, and over the years he had developed quite a passable Glaswegian accent. He was renowned for trading in goods such as watches that would cease to function as soon as you had left the harbour. After two or three incidences of these dodgy transactions, I cooked up a plan of retribution, and this is how it played out. The favourite monthly cigarette issue in those days were John Players. These were issued in fifties in flat black tins sealed in cellophane. Over the months I was on the boat I had accumulated eight tins. The cellophane I carefully removed and when the tins were empty, I refilled them with mash potatoes. I did this just a day or two prior to reaching Aden, since I did not want any strange aromas being emitted. After filling the eight tins very carefully, I resealed them in the saved cellophane. So, as far as anyone else was concerned, I had four hundred cigarettes with which to barter with McGregor.

We arrived in Aden and after a very short period, out rowed McGregor. I had a good look over his cargo and spied a very nice grey silk shirt. I greeted him with: "Hello McGregor, I've got some cigarettes for payment. Are you OK with that"? He replied: "Aye laddie, nay bother". I said: "I will give you two hundred cigarettes for that grey shirt". Mc Gregor said: "Laddie dinna mess with me, it's worth six hundred". Well this went on for a while until we settled for four hundred. He then threw a rope on board to which was tied a straw basket. I filled the basket with my eight tins and lowered them down to him. He unloaded the tins and sent up the shirt.

We were about to sail and the gangway that had been hung on the boat was raised. I was leaning on the handrail still looking at McGregor and thinking: 'that's it mate, pay-back time'. Then I noticed him removing one of the cellophane covers. I guess he must have fancied a smoke, and of course, in doing so he discovered my little ploy. He started ripping off the rest of the cellophane covers. He looked up and saw me looking at him, and started swearing in the most profane way, but this time there was no trace of the Glaswegian accent! Then he drew his finger across his throat and said: "You come back next trip and I will keel you English Peeg". I replied by giving him the thumbs up with one hand and a reverse Churchillian salute with the other, whilst at the same time giving a fair rendition of Rule Britannia.

As mentioned above, Aden being in the Red sea, the temperature was always very high and of course, in those days there was no such thing as air conditioning. This meant that the only way of cooling the cabins was via wind chutes, which were fixed to the portholes and protruded on the outside. The idea was that they would catch any wind that was available and direct it back into the cabin, which was not very efficient, especially when the sea was flat calm.

Not So Smart

After leaving Aden and sailing through the Suez Canal, our next port of call was Genoa in Italy, a place I really liked. On my first night ashore two mates and I were strolling along the main street, when we were approached by a man. He pointed to the three off us, asking "English?" We replied: "Yes". His next question was: "Do you have any Ronson cigarette lighters to sell? In those days, a good Ronson was very sought after. I said: "I may have one, but how much are you willing to pay?" "Let me see it" he said. Now, I knew my Ronson was a nice one, and he gave it the once over and said: "I will give you five thousand Lira", and at seventeen hundred to the pound that was a pretty good price. So I agreed. Then he said: "I have only got a ten thousand Lira note. Do you have change? I said I did and gave him a five thousand Lira note and the Ronson lighter. I expect the reader is in front of me by now, because when I went to pay for a round of drinks with the ten thousand lire note, the waiter said: "This no good it's drachma Greek money". The rate of exchange then was forty thousand drachma to the pound, so my Greek note was worth about five shillings. It's funny, but as life goes on, what goes around comes around. Do you recall the time when I pinched that ten shilling note from the American soldier? Also, more recently, having had McGregor over. Well, it seemed to be my turn to become the victim. Nevertheless, it infuriated me that this supposedly, street wise, self-opinionated idiot could be so easily duped. Furthermore, to rub salt into the wound, prior to Genoa our previous port had been Piraeus in Greece.

Promotion

I was now eighteen and no longer a boy rating. As a fully-fledged Steward, the next boat I joined was a lovely looking craft called the Braemar Castle. She was a seventeen thousand ton cargo/passenger liner, and she belonged to the Union Castle line.

`My first job in this new role was as a crew messman. I went to my cabin and began to unpack. The first thing I removed was a nice new white shirt, and underneath that were four pairs of socks, which caused me to have a very long pause. The thought that went through my head was Johnny boy you've arrived; respectability at last. My mind went back to Jersey Road in the war, when I had only one pair of knee length socks, which after a while developed large holes at the heels. My shoes were too big so my heels were exposed with every pace I took. Even as a small child this really embarrassed me, so to overcome this I would pull the sock down so that the hole was now concealed inside my shoe. But of course another hole would soon occur in the back part of the sock I had pulled down, so I would repeat the procedure just one more time. By now my knee length socks had become ankle length. Of course, this would now lead to the pulled down socks filling up my shoes, so to counter this I would cut the front part of the sock off. On seeing what I had done, my Mum said: "Don't you ever get run over because I could never live with the shame". At that time, Glen Miller's famous swing band had a hit called 'String of Pearls'. I had another version called 'Sock of Holes'.

I gradually progressed through the catering ranks, at first becoming a tourist class waiter. I had joined another Union Castle ship called the Warwick Castle, which carried both tourist and first class passengers. I had a table of eighteen situated right at the end of the dining saloon, which meant that all of my training at the Gravesend Sea Training school on the correct mannerisms when serving a passenger, took a back seat. My first modification came when I was serving soup, I had by now obtained a big white enamel Jug, which I filled with the soup of the day, I would stand at the end of my aircraft carrier (that's what I called my table) and call out "Right, who wants soup, put your hands up!" Then I would go round and fill the already laid plates. I continued this 'hands up' question and answering procedure on each course of the meal, much to the amusement of the other waiters, and even some of my passengers. But alas, one day the Head Waiter stood aghast at my unusual style. He called me to one side and asked if I had I ever waited on tables before. I said I had, to my Mum and Dad at home". I asked if he was sure about wanting me to revert to the time wasting methods used by the other waiters, which would mean that by the time the food was served, it would be cold. By now, his face was beginning to take on a nice shade of red, and in a very quiet but slightly menacing tone he said: "Ringwood this is the Union Castle line, and this is how we do it, and if you do not like our methods then I will kick your arse all the way to the Galley, where you will become a scullion, and then your job will be to wash and clean all the pots and pans used by the cooks". Well, this put a whole new light on the matter, so I apologised profusely and said: "I am sorry Sir and I will amend my style accordingly". He gave me a funny old look and said: "You better have boy, because from now on I will be watching you".

Most passengers were a delight, but now and again you would get an awkward one. This was in the days of apartheid, and on one occasion there was a passenger who was white and South African, and clearly used to getting attention by clicking his fingers. I was just passing to the rear of him when, without looking at me, he lifted up his arm clicked his finger and thumb, whilst at the same time pointing to an empty plate, indicating that he wanted it moved. I did not respond until he did it again. Then I grabbed his finger and thumb and gave it a good twist. He yelped, saying

"What the hell are you doing? I replied: "No Sir, the question is what the hell are you doing? If you want my attention then you call out 'waiter' and I will respond". The rest of the seventeen passengers were nodding in agreement to what I had just said. However, because of his yelp the Head Waiter came bounding over. The aggrieved passenger told the Head Waiter that I had just assaulted him. The Head Waiter replied: "What did he actually do?" "He twisted my thumb and finger together" said the man. "And what Sir, were you actually doing at that time, which caused the waiter to carry out this action?" The man replied "I was just clicking my finger and thumb together to get his attention". I saw the Head Waiter stiffen. "Really sir: Then I have to inform you that if you use that method of the gaining the attention of any of my staff, you will always get a very negative response. However, if my steward did do what you said, then he will be severely reprimanded". He then asked me for my understanding of the alleged assault. Of course, I denied it and said: "I may have brushed by his hand, but I do not agree to what he reported I had said". All of the above, whether rightly or wrongly, was discussed in front of the other passengers. The Head Waiter then asked an open question of the table: "Did anyone else see what happened?" One of the male passengers said that it was more or less as the waiter described; that he saw the passenger clicking his fingers at the waiter, who then pushed his hand away and whispered something in his ear. Other passengers nodded in agreement. By now the irate passenger was beginning to see the error of his ways and said: "Okay let's leave it there, but I want to be moved to another table". This request was carried out promptly, much to the relief of the other passengers. More evidence if needed to suggest that he wasn't a very pleasant man.

Shortly afterwards, the Head Waiter called me over and said: "You need to be careful son. You were on very thin ice there for a while." I thanked him, but pointed out that the passenger really was a prat!

MV Taranaki

The happiest and best boat I ever sailed on was a cargo boat called the MV Taranaki. She belonged to the Shaw Saville Line, and was built in 1928. She weighed nearly eleven thousand tons and her top speed was eleven knots, which is about fifteen miles an hour. Without doubt, she was a gracious old lady.

This trip lasted for nearly seven months, in total. We travelled right around the world, out through the Panama Canal and home through the Suez Canal. Over my first three years at sea, I made sure that every trip was on a different run. But this was the trip that led me to the perfect place: the country that I could live in if I ever wanted to move away from England and live somewhere else. It is known by its inhabitants and most seafarers who have been there, as The Land of the Long White Cloud. Of course, I am referring to the Wonderful New Zealand. I will give a brief explanation of how different it was for seamen in those days compared to what happens now. Normally, to load a cargo and to get ships in good order before sailing from UK ports it could take three weeks to a month. On arrival in New Zealand you might call at up to six different ports so you could be on their coast for up to eight weeks. Nowadays, because of containerisation, where all the cargoes are encased in huge metal boxes, they are carried to the ports by road or rail then loaded on to the boats by huge modern cranes built for that purpose. It means that a boat of considerable size can be turned around in twenty four hours. Can you imagine that a trip from the UK to New Zealand could take three to four weeks? Then you might find that the next day you are on our way home again, with hardly a chance to sink a pint let alone make an acquaintance from someone of the opposite sex. No wonder the Merchant Navy I knew no longer exists.

Practically every week I receive mail, inviting my wife and myself to cruise to far off climes. I have to say that the liners on offer look no more like ships than a fly in the air. Rather, they resemble a block of flats with a sharp front and a blunt end. One of the trips on offer was for a forty one day cruise, and the top price was thirteen thousand pounds. Well, there was I, in the prime of my life, sailing away for seven months at a time, being given pretty good food, and there was beer on board if we wanted, albeit with certain restrictions. I was in the company of great fellas, calling at exotic ports, and getting paid at the same time. Who do you think had the best deal?

Let's return to the Taranaki. Yes, she was an old lady, but when I joined her the crews' accommodation had just been refurbished and it was just two to a cabin. My cabin mate was called Alf and my job on this occasion was steward to the engineering officers. I always preferred these to the deck officers, since sometimes they had a bit of an attitude, as already illustrated.

I remember one night in particular. It was about eight o' clock, and I had just finished giving my engineers their dinner. I decided to go on deck and have a smoke. We were right in the middle of the Indian Ocean, the sea was very calm and the only sounds that could be heard were the throb of the engines and the sea breaking over the bow. There was no one else on deck except me. I looked up and the sky was totally covered with what seemed to be thousands of stars. It was absolutely beautiful, and the sense of peace that I experienced at that moment I had never known before or since. It was like being in a massive cathedral with the heavens as the ceiling and I knew from that moment that somewhere in the future, my life would change.

Our first port of call in New Zealand was Auckland. This was the era of the Teddy Boys in the UK, a style I didn't really like but which I thought I would try and adapt to my taste, as outlined below. At that time, the Tatler magazine often featured Edwardian clothes, and one example ensemble was a three piece suit with a double breasted waistcoat. I took the magazine to my Tailor, Lew Rose of East Ham, and asked him if could make a suit as featured. He jumped at the idea, and made an excellent job of the tailoring. The next item purchased was a small brimmed brown Derby hat and a pair of very high quality shoes: all in all there was a pretty close resemblance to the Tatler rigout. Reader, if you are wondering whether my clothes had the desired effect with the New Zealand opposite sex (now whatever I say is going to sound like boasting) suffice it to say that the money I spent on the attire was well worth it.

I have found that whenever there are a good number of men together it cannot always be plain sailing and one indication of this involved my lifelong pal called Frank. He was not like the rest of us who came from London. , Frank came from Henley on Thames and wasn't quite so streetwise. Anyway, somehow we acquired a small kitten, which I was teasing by putting my hand under a seat cushion, with just my fingers exposed, and which I then wiggled about. On seeing this, the kitten would spring forward whilst at the same time, I would pull my fingers down, and the kitten would hit its head on the back of the chair. Frank wasn't happy with this and told me to stop it. In retrospect he was right, but I said that if the kitten didn't enjoy it he would stop, and so I did it again. This time Frank said: "That's it John I have had enough, get up on deck". Well for those who don't know, this is a challenge to a fight. I said: "Sorry Frank, I don't want to fight you mate". Well, I think he took this as a sign of fear, but he could not have been more wrong, because he then said: "Come on tough guy let's get it on". So up on deck we went, and as expected he came in arms and fists flailing in all directions and missing completely, the desired target. I pinned his arms to his side in a clinch and said: "Let's stop mate, I really don't want to do this. You are my mate. Come on, let's forget it". But he insisted and broke away, and again came flying in at me. I swerved to one side and threw a very heavy right that landed on his nose causing a severe bleed. That did it; fight over. This might sound soft, but I broke down and cried because this was the last thing I had ever wanted to happen. I thought the world of this kid. Frank and I still meet some sixty years on, and his nose which is slightly hooked has a little bend to starboard. When we meet he points out to the assembled company that it was his best mate in the world who did that.

When we left New Zealand finally, our next port of call was Aden for refuelling. Because of our very slow speed it took nearly three weeks to get there, and except for a brief glimpse of Australia that was the only bit of land we saw before arriving in McGregor land. In total, our trip took seven months and on entering the English Channel all of our thoughts were of home and love ones. However, Jack Dash, who was a leading light in the Docker's union, had other ideas, and for whatever reason called for strike action in the Royal Docks. He was successful and the docks came to a standstill for nearly three weeks. On arriving at the mouth of the Thames, just off South End Pier, the engines stopped and the anchor was dropped and that's where we stayed until the strike was over. It's true to say Jack Dash was not the most popular man amongst the crew of the Taranaki. Still, after travelling all around the world, the best sun tan I have ever had was during those weeks under an English summer sun. Not too long ago my wife Brenda and I went to Southend and caught the train to the end of the Pier. As I sat there in the twilight of my life, I looked out at the sea and remembered my wonderful shipmates and the old Taranaki, which had been anchored there so long ago.

Now that I had sampled New Zealand, there was no other place that I wanted to go, and the two shipping companies that met my needs, were The New Zealand and Shaw Saville lines. My last four trips on the Shaw Saville line were as a first class waiter, which was a role I really took to. I never had any trouble at all with any of my passengers. These were old school gentry, there were none of the airs and graces associated with 'new money': they appeared to be a class act, effortlessly.

My last trip was on the Gothic. I joined her just after Her Majesty the Queen had sailed on her whilst carrying out a Commonwealth tour. The Gothic, still painted white, was a cargo/passenger liner not very big at just over seventeen thousand tons, and her passengers were all first class. In addition to being a waiter, I was in charge of the dining saloon silver, and I took a great deal of pride in ensuring it was kept in bright and shiny condition. I had a round table of six which consisted of the Ship's Doctor, a Lord and Lady and their daughter and a husband and wife. I believe the husband held a high position in New Zealand Airways. Without boasting I hope, my round table, especially when laid up for dinner at night, looked a work of art. The effect was achieved by meticulous spacing between the cutlery, glasses and crockery, and coupled with the finest silver from my store, it even drew a compliment from the Head Waiter: praise indeed.

Fifteen:
Dock Work

Between trips, it was my habit to get casual work in the docks in ship repair. This was made possible because my Dad had returned to work in the dock as a ship's scaler, having left the Merchant Navy. My job was as a fitter's mate, but being casual, I still had to assemble on the cobbles, waiting to be chosen by the charge hand. I was picked fairly often, partly because of my dad's influence but also because my mate Ricky, another seaman, and I were known as hard grafters, and reputed to be good with the heavy hammer. Without getting too technical, the big hammer (called a Monday hammer) was used to hit a very large spanner, attached to a massive nut which had to be dismantled from a piston in the ship's engine. The hammer weighed twenty eight pounds, and Ricky and I would have a competition to see who could swing the most without resting. We were both little fellas, weighing no more than nine stones, but we were pretty strong for our size and weight. It was called a Monday hammer because you were too knackered to use it on Tuesday. The job entailed getting into a pretty small place under the engine, and on one particular occasion I thought I had taken all the necessary tools to get in there, only to find that I had left a spanner up on the gantry.

One of our gang was a gay man called George. But at the time he would be described as 'a queer'. He was a great guy, but loved to tease and wind me up. Moreover, although he was very camp in his mannerisms, below the surface there was a VERY tough hombre weighing in at about eighteen stones. One story goes that during the war, George was a barmaid/bouncer in the Bridge House Pub in Canning Town and on one evening three American soldiers became very drunk and wanted to fight everybody. George put down his drying up cloth and came out into the drinking area. He went up to the soldiers and in his very effeminate voice told them to behave or he would have to throw them out. They responded by copying George's voice and mannerisms whilst also starting to throw punches. Witnesses have said that within a matter of seconds, George knocked the three of them spark out, and not content with that, he draped all three over the top of the pub's upright piano, picked up his cloth and went back behind the bar.

Now back to the episode of the forgotten spanner. George was standing next to it so I asked him to hand it down to me, to which he replied,: "No I am not your bleeding skivvy". I said: "Come on George, don't mess about, give me that f*****g spanner". His response was: "Piss off. Come up and get it yourself". I said: "Okay. I will come and get it and then I'll sort you out". With that, I clambered out, went up to him and said: "Right Georgie boy, I have had enough. Get up on that bleeding deck". With that he smirked: "Okay tough guy, let's go". On the way up from the engine room I could see he was shaking his head and laughing, which wound me up even more but at the same time a reality check was beginning to kick in and I thought 'Shit, what's got into you, he will take you apart'. Fortunately, my saviour appeared in the form of my Dad, just as we were arriving on the deck. He asked what was going on, so I told him. His response was to grab me by the scruff of neck and push me back to the door leading to the engine room, and with a final shove he pushed me through saying: "Now get down below and behave your bleeding self you stupid little sod". But just before I went I turned around and said to George: "Think yourself lucky mate that this ain't gone any further". He replied, still laughing: "Ooh I do sailor, I do." Then he turned to my Dad and said: "Isn't he the bold one?"

Over the following years George became a very close friend of my family, and one night I reminded him about the above incident when I nearly made a complete prat of myself. Bearing in mind that at that time, I weighed just over nine stones against George's eighteen I said: "George, just say it had kicked off. Would you have beaten me up?" He replied "Nah, what do you take me for, a complete liberty taker? Of course not, anyway with just one punch I would have knocked you over the side. What I would have done, was to put both hands on your head to keep you at arm's length and just let you punch yourself out, but thanks to your old man it got sorted anyway". "Much to my relief" I said.

A few years later, when my two sons were quite young, George came round to my house one Sunday morning. He was wearing a pair of shorts that were both very short and very tight. On passing the boys, who were playing in the front garden, he said: "Hello boys, say good morning to your Aunty George". They looked at one another with very puzzled expressions on their faces. When George left, my eldest Terry said: "Dad, he asked us to call him aunty, but he's a man". I replied: "Boys, I will explain that when you are a little older". George came from one of the toughest families in Canning Town, and I said to him one day: "How did your Dad respond when he saw that you were queer?" He replied: "He horsewhipped me". I said "It didn't do much good mate did it?" He replied: "No. No I liked it".

The charge hand of our gang was named Bill. But he had a large bump on the back of his head, so that's what he was known as. He had a younger brother called Rigby, who was known to like a drink or two. He was also the gang's runner, or gofer to use a more modern term. On one particular Friday, Bump on the head sent Rigby to go and collect the gang's wages. Friday evening came, but there was no sign of Rigby or our wages. Contact was made with the main office which confirmed that the wages were given to Rigby mid-afternoon. By this time we were getting a bit fed up and let management know it. They concurred, that there must be a reasonable explanation for the non-delivery of the money, but in the meantime another set of wages was made up and sent to us. The reasonable explanation, discovered a week later, turned out to be that Rigby was in a rehab clinic in Cornwall, minus our wages but with a very bad hangover. In later life I became a Health and Safety consultant, and part of my role was to carry out risk assessments. Without doubt, the decision to send Rigby to collect our wages, would have been allocated a high risk value.

Another anecdote from this time concerns Ricky, whom I have already mentioned, and myself, whilst we were working in the ship repairer's yard/factory on the Isle of Dogs. This was at a time when there were no ships on which to work on. Next to our place of work was what we thought to be a derelict warehouse. Being curious we decided to give it the once over one lunchtime. We gained access by climbing through a fairly small fanlight window but once inside we could not see much because most of the windows had been boarded up. However, in one room we found a small canvas bag. When we opened it we found what looked like a hoard of large jewels. Rick said "I think we have got somebody's swag here. Let's get out and have a look". Then he said: "What's that noise?" I said: "It sounds like the whistle on a boiling kettle", which it was. What we figured was that it probably belonged to a watchman who was looking after the place. Without a doubt he would have heard us prowling around and was waiting for the chance to telephone the police about our presence. So we legged it through the door that we found open. Once we were a safe distance from the warehouse we opened the bag, only to find that our jewels turned out to be ornate coloured glass draw handles. I suspect that what we had found was a salesman's sample bag, so instead of retiring to the good life, it was back to reality and the Monday Hammer!

In terms of more general observations about life in the docks at that time, what is often not fully appreciated is the role women played, especially during the War. Most dock workers will remember the women who drove around the vans carrying hot drinks and food both mid-morning and afternoon. These breaks were known by us all as 'mobiles'. However, another group of female workers was not so widely known: many of the shipping companies employed them just prior to the ship sailing, to clean the inside of the boat from top to bottom. They were fondly called 'ship scrubbers'. One of the boats I was on was due for this cleaning ritual and I recognised two of these ladies as they came on board. One was a neighbour named Mrs O, and the other was an old school mate called Sheila. After a brief chat Mrs O said: "I am having a bit of a house party tonight. Would you like to come?, "You bet." I replied. I duly attended what turned out to be a good old East End knees up. The only things missing from her house were a funnel and port holes. Everything else was there: all the cutlery, towels, curtains, table cloths and sheets and small carpets all instantly recognisable by being clearly marked by numerous shipping companies. "Done alright there mate." I said. She replied: "Yeah, perks of the job". Regrettably, Sheila and her husband were among the victims when the Ronan Point tower block collapsed.

Sixteen:
The Army

National Service was a requirement for all young men, until nineteen sixty one which meant that at the age of eighteen or 21, if you were an apprentice, you were conscripted to serve for two years in one of the armed services, provided that you passed a medical. As far as I was concerned, as long as I served ten uninterrupted years in the Merchant Navy, then I would be exempt. In my case that would be from sixteen to twenty six. I had already overstayed my leave by a few weeks, working in the docks and earning very good money. I knew I was chancing my arm, hoping the powers to be would not notice, but of course they did. On arriving home one night, my mum was waving a brown envelope at me saying: "You are not going to like this one little bit, Johnny boy". Wow! Was she right! The letter informed me that I had been conscripted and was to go to Russell Square, in London for a medical. Sod this for a lark, I though. So the next morning, I went straight down to the Shipping Federation, put my Seamen's book over the counter and said: "Ready to sail again mate. What's on offer?" He looked my name up, pushed the book back to me and said: "For you sailor, nothing. You have been called up haven't you?" I replied: "Well, yes, but surely we can work something out. He said: "No son, once you have been notified, that's it". Well that was it. I was gutted. I really did not want to play soldiers.

So, on the allocated date I duly attended Russell Square for a medical. In front of me in the queue was a fella who looked like Mr Universe. In he went and after a short time he came out again. I asked him how he got on. He replied that he failed. I looked down at my puny nine stone and thought to myself, whoopee if he's failed I am never going to pass. So in I went. After a very brief examination by the doctor, and a cough, he said to the nurse "Passed A1". I said: "Passed. Are you sure? Have another look, doc". But he said: "That's enough on your way".

Then I was interviewed by another army officer, who asked what I did I for a living? I told him that I was a merchant seaman, and he replied: "Surely you are exempt in that profession?" I replied that he was said was right, but that I had overstayed my leave whilst working in the docks, and had been called up. He asked what my job was in the docks. I said that I worked on ships engines. Then he said: "I think you are just the man we are looking for. We have some small craft that need maintaining in Singapore. Do you think you would be a suitable candidate?". Now, I have very fond memories of Singapore, so I readily agreed. He seemed pleased by this and said he would be in touch.

When I got home I was full of it, saying that I thought I had cracked it and that Singapore would not be so bad. But my Dad was sitting in his chair, quietly reading his paper. After a while he peered over the top and said: "What's the opposite to the sea son?" "Land" I said. "You are right boy and that's' where you will be. On land, in the bloody infantry", said Dad. Naturally, he was proved right. I received a letter stating that I was to report to Her Majesty's Tower of London, on 5 December, to join the Royal Fusiliers' City of London Regiment.

The Tower of London

When the cold winter's day arrived I went through the main gates of the Tower, not really looking forward to it one little bit. As I was ambling across the cobble stones in front of what turned out to be the barracks, a very large man with an even larger voice called out: "Are you one of the new intake people?" I replied that I was. Still in a loud voice he boomed: "Well young man, you will quickly learn this hallowed ground is my parade ground and this will be the last time you will be allowed to stroll across it. Do you understand?" I gave a little shrug and said: "Yes I guess so". This loud voice was the first of many I was going to encounter for the next ten weeks.

The first thing that happened was that we were split up into platoons. The one to which I was assigned was called Mons after the famous Battle. Then we were issued with uniforms which consisted of a battle dress, overcoat, boots gaiters shirts, beret, tie, pyjamas and tin helmet.

Accompanying, this kit were pouches, knapsack and a heavy buckled belt. The last three items had to be coated with a substance named blanco.

During the next three weeks my feet hardly touched the ground. Everything was at the double, we were taught how to clean our kit and polish our boots: I will dwell on this because it is an art to get it right. When issued, the leather boots have a mottled effect, so this has to go. This is achieved by putting a heavy coat of black polish on the toes and heels, then heating the handle of a fork over a gas flame to a very high temperature, which you then press all over areas where the polish has been applied until the mottled surface is flattened. One recruit overdid the heating of the fork, and burnt the stitching that held the toe cap onto the rest of the boot. The boot sprung open on parade when he banged his foot whilst coming to attention, which brought a wry comment from the sergeant, that the soldier should 'take it easy since those boots are supposed to last two years'. Of course, he knew what had happened. To achieve the very glossy polish effect, you have to apply a small amount of polish to the surface of the boot: then with a soft linen cloth you work the polish in with small circular movements of the index finger until it is absorbed. This is followed by spitting (I now use a dab of cold water) onto the same area and repeating the process. If you persevere then in a very short period your efforts will be rewarded. The secret is to keep the amount of polish and spit to a minimum each time. Some sixty years later all of my shoes are still highly polished. I even find the method explained very relaxing!

I adapted pretty quickly to this new regime. It was not a lot different to my time served in the M.N. In essence, it meant conforming to a new set of rules and practices, but the one thing that was totally different was trying to get us all to a high standard of fitness, and being a heavy smoker and a dock working, drinking man this felt like a hard target for me to achieve. However, somehow I reached the required level. Much to my surprise, during the first week at the Tower I was made Squad leader of the Mons platoon. I figured it was because of the age difference: I was four years older than the rest of the recruits. To some of them I become like an older brother because it was easy for me to adapt, but for some of the others it wasn't and they found it hard to cope, especially when as an individual they were singled out for not getting a point quick enough from an irate corporal or sergeant. After three weeks we were beginning to gel, especially on the parade ground and you could begin to feel a sense of pride happening. In my opinion, when issued, the uniform at that time was possibly the scruffiest in existence, but I did notice that with a few subtle changes, it could look fairly smart.

Our lieutenant, Mike Warren was a very smart and capable officer. He was also quite a good looking fella. One evening, he came into our room in his full dress uniform. One of the boys asked if he was going somewhere special and he said that he was, as a matter of fact, and with a little wink he left us. Another of the boys was looking out of the window onto the parade ground and noticed two very attractive young ladies waiting by the exit door through which our officer was to depart and in no time, all of us were at the window gaping at these lovely creatures. What must be taken into account is that we had been denied female company for nearly a month by this stage and frustration was setting in. On seeing the young beauties our man kissed each of them on the cheek and sauntered off with one on each arm and he had our instant respect from then onwards. He was also an excellent field officer: he never expected us to do anything that he had not first demonstrated, and in most cases was far better in carrying it out than any of us.

We were allowed two days leave on the fourth week, and to tell you the truth, what with my beret resembling a 78 record disk and wearing this khaki, furry uniform, I felt a complete prat as I boarded the train at Tower Hill Station for the journey home. But, my girlfriend Brenda, who was later to become my wife, was a dress maker, so on my instructions, we started to work together on restyling this monstrosity. I had a good idea about what to do because I had studied the adaptions that one of the smartest corporal's had made. One of the most risky actions was carried out with a very hot iron. To get rid of the hairy finish on the cloth you had to scorch it lightly, which made the hairs brittle. Then the cloth needed to be rubbed with a half crown coin, which gave the material a very smooth finish. My next task was to go to the nearest army surplus store, where I purchased a small Belgian beret and two Canadian army shirts. Then I boiled my tie in milk so that it finished up a nice cream colour.

When boarding the train back to the Tower on Monday, I felt a totally different man: the old smart Johnny Ringwood was back. Before going back to the barracks we had to assemble for a head count, and with my newly adapted appearance I stood out like a sore thumb. The sergeant who was carrying out the head count paused when he came to me, and said that he never knew we had a trained soldier amongst this intake. Then he asked my corporal if I was a trained soldier. He replied that I was not. Turning back to me he said: "Do you know that although you look very smart, these adaptions you have made are not allowed until you have completed your basic training. So you will be charged with misconduct and dealt with accordingly. But first go to the stores and with the exception of your boots, belt and gaiters, hand the rest in and tell the storeman, under my orders, that you are to be reissued, at your own cost, with a replacement standard recruit's uniform. Part of my punishment was the loss of some home leave. That was the first time I tried to shortcut the system and I can honestly say that after numerous attempts, I never beat the army once. Not all was lost, however, because I made a pact with the fella in the stores to return my stuff once I had finished basic training. Once again, I think the currency was cigarettes.

Apart from the Tower, where the regime was all about drills inspections and basic keep fit, there was another depot in Purfleet, where the training was more in line with action in the field. The barracks dated from the Second World War and were similar to Nissan huts. In mid- January they were very cold, with the only heat coming from two pot belly cast iron fires, fuelled by coal and positioned in the middle of the room. I think I felt the cold more than most, having missed seven English winters whist serving in the M.N. So again, it was time to improve the situation. This was achieved by bringing from home, my Mum's two bar electric-fire and fortunately there was an electrical socket outlet next to my bed. I kept the fire out of notice until our corporal had done his final rounds, then I plugged it in for the night. The next morning I awoke with a start thinking my face was on fire, only to find that the corporal had positioned the fire just a few inches from my head. He enquired: "Warm enough for you Sir? "I don't want any of my guests getting cold". Then he exploded. Pulling the plug out of the socket, he picked up the fire and threw it against the wall, saying: "Well, you won't be using that again will you? OK squad leader what have you got to say for yourself?" I replied: "Well corporal, I thought I was showing a bit of initiative in warming the place up a bit". He screamed: "Initiative, "initiative… soldier the only equipment you will ever use in this man's army is that which has been issued by Her Majesty the Queen. Do you understand you little frozen turd?" "Fully" I replied. "Good." He said. "But you are still on a charge of stealing the army's electricity".

Another cold related incident happened on the rifle range where we were attempting to hit the targets with our Lee Enfield rifles. When my turn came, I lay down on the ground, took aim and was just about to fire, when the corporal said: "Stop!" I felt him prodding the bottom of my leg with a stick and he said: "That's a very serious skin condition you have Ringwood." I had not realised that the bottom of my trousers had ridden up over my gaiters, exposing my blue and white striped pyjamas which I had left on to counter the cold. "Oh dear me" said the corporal, "just as I was beginning to think I was turning you all into hardened, trained fighting men I find we have someone with a soft centre". "Sorry corporal" I said. "But I feel the cold"." Sorry, SORRY! (He had a habit of repeating himself) he shouted. "You will be if I kick you up the arse, you pathetic excuse for a man let alone a soldier". I was beginning to get the idea that he didn't like me very much. I thought to myself that's good, I have only been in this mob a few weeks and I have been whacked all over the place, and how am I going to explain to my Mum about her fire?'. It goes without saying I was no longer the squad leader.

Another thing I found a little frustrating was the routine you had to perform to collect your weekly wages. You had to form an orderly queue and when it was your turn you had to march smartly up to the table, coming to an abrupt halt and salute (longest way up shortest way down), hold your hand out and receive twenty eight shillings. The week before I joined the army, my wages in the docks had been twenty eight pounds. One Monday morning I came back from leave feeling a little the worse for wear, having had a very heavy previous night on the gin and tonics. Our first session was on the parade ground carrying out arms drill: it was a bitterly cold day and I thought to myself I have had enough of this and pretended to faint. I was then carried to the medical orderlies to recover. After about fifteen minutes my Sergeant came in and told the orderly to leave. He sat on the bed and said: "Ringwood I have got your number. If you think you can work your ticket and get out of the army think again. Ron and Reginald Cray did it but you won't". (The Cray twins were also conscripted into the Royal Fusiliers). Actually he had got it wrong; the thought had never entered my mind. My attitude was keep your head down in the future and soldier on.

After ten weeks our families were invited to the Tower to see how the army had turned their degenerates into trained fighting men. Part of the passing out parade was in the area in front of the barracks, and the man in charge was the feared but highly respected Regimental Sergeant Major Tiny Duran. By now, much to the sergeants' and corporals' credit, we carried out the drills in a pretty smart fashion. All of us, including the guests went into a large hall where a group of our intake was to demonstrate how physically fit we had become. One of the demonstrations was to climb up ropes that were suspended from the ceiling, and among the five picked to carry out this feat was a good mate of mine called Ron. Halfway up the rope the strain became too much and he passed wind, which was both long and loud. After a stunned silence a very embarrassed Ron descended and said sorry about that, and then one of the sergeants said: "That's all right son but next time let us know when you are going to include a fanfare in the programme".

Our intake was then posted to Dover for another three weeks to finalise our training. We could now call ourselves fully trained Fusiliers. During our time at Dover we were put into different companies, according to our various abilities, and I had already given this matter some thought. Throughout the day bugle calls were used to signal different events, such as waking up and mealtimes. It so happened that my dad, who was a pretty good trumpet player had also introduced me to the instrument, and after speaking to a couple of fellas in the Corps of drums, I learned that playing an instrument was not a bad job. So, I had an interview with the Drum Major, a really nice guy called Dickie Rose, who asked: "Can you play an instrument?" I replied: "I can knock a tune out on a trumpet". "Can you now? Well give me five notes on this bugle" he said. This was not as easy as it sounds because the mouthpiece is slightly different from a trumpet. His response to my efforts was: "Not bad. With a bit of practice I think you will be okay, but along with the bugle you will have to learn to play the fife, which is a type of flute. Do you think you can do it?" I said I would certainly give it my best shot.

So I became a member of the Royal Fusiliers Corps of Drums, a role which gave me a real sense of pride and enjoyment. Very shortly after the battalion posted abroad, half went to Bahrein and half to Kenya. The Drums was part of the Headquarter Company, and we were fortunate enough to be going to Kenya.

Our trip was on a troopship called the Dunera. The food was good but the accommodation consisting of rows and rows of metal bunks was pretty basic. I always found amusing that we had to lay to attention on these whenever roll call was made. We looked like corpses laying there. Before leaving the ship we were issued with tropical clothing, which was a lot more comfortable than our battle dress.

On arriving at Mombasa, we disembarked and boarded a train bound for Nairobi, a distance of nearly three hundred miles. We passed through some glorious landscapes, which was very new to me, because as a seaman, who had travelled the world all I normally saw was the nearest bar, and the rest I will leave to your imagination! From Nairobi we were to travel on three ton Bedford troop lorries to our final destination which was called Gill Gill, and which is approximately six thousand feet above sea level. It was in an area called the White Highlands, and it was stunningly beautiful. Our hut was right on the perimeter of the camp overlooking the Rift Valley, and in the mornings we would be level with the clouds so that the valley looked as if it was covered in a giant white table cloth. Every now and then, a bird would emerge giving the whole scene a magical appearance. Wild animals, especially baboons would sometimes come into the camp. These night time visitors were normally found loitering around the cookhouse. On one particular night, I was on guard duty and armed only with a pickaxe handle. On passing the cookhouse my mate who was on duty with me said: "There is something in there Johnny". So I said we should go in and have a look. I spied what I thought was a dog in the corner with a joint of meat in its mouth and on seeing me, it started to growl. I raised my handle in self-defence and approached it, hoping to scare it away, but the growling grew louder. Then, my mate said suddenly: "Back off John it's a bleeding hyena". It appeared he knew more about animals than I did, because he said, after we had legged it, that a hyena when cornered is one of the most dangerous animals alive. They never taught me that at the Tower.

The Mau Mau problem in Kenya was coming to an end, but on occasion a number of us would still be sent to farms owned by white Kenyans for a weekend stay. In the Drums were three black guys from St Lucia, and they were included in the group on one of these visits. On arriving, the farmer said "They can't stay here". I replied: "Is that so? Well let me tell you, mate. These three men are not only my comrades but also members of Her Majesty's British Army, and if they cannot stay, then neither can we." With that, we all got back on the lorry and returned to camp. I was hauled over the coals and was told I should have allowed him to explain. I replied: "I am sorry Sir but that is not the way I see it. It seems to me to be a basic case of discrimination". It was noted, however, that my three mates were never again sent on these excursions.

I absolutely fell in love with this part of Kenya. Because we were so high it never got too hot, and of a night time it was not unknown to have a blanket on your bed. We spent nearly a year there and on occasions would go to Mombasa Nayeli beach for a week's leave, swimming in the Indian Ocean: it was Paradise.

On one occasion Her Majesty the Queen Mother made a visit to Kenya, and in her honour our Corps of Drums carried out a Beating of the Retreat. This was held in another beautiful spot called Niavasha. After we had finished we were lined up and presented to her Majesty, who asked us where we come from. When it came to my turn I said "Custom House. It's in East End". Her reply was "Oh I know Custom House". I replied "I know you do Mam. You and His majesty the King visited us during the blitz". Our Drum Major was well pleased about how we carried out the Retreat, and treated us all to a drink. It was a very nice gesture, and I think it confirms my impression that he was a nice bloke. By now I was becoming quite proficient at playing the bugle, and on one evening it came to ten o' clock and it was time to play the last post. There is the army way of playing it where each note has to be of a certain length and at the right pitch. However, my interpretation meant taking a slightly different approach. I liked to play with feeling, as is appropriate for such a serious call, so some of the notes I would play loud, and some softer. Also, I would pause a tiny fraction between notes. I felt that at the end of this particular call I had never played as well. I guess it goes back to my love of good music. After dismissing the guard the officer came over to me and said: "Well played drummer". About half an hour later, whilst sitting in the guard room with the rest of the fellas on duty for the night, a batman (servant) from the officers' mess came in with a gin and tonic on a tray. On seeing me, he passed on the compliments of the officers mess, and handed me the drink, which certainly seemed to me to be an incentive to play as well again in the future.

Regrettably, this first stay in Kenya came to an abrupt end. It was because conflict had erupted in the Persian Gulf and our boys in Bahrein were put on stand by for action. Most of us Kenya boys were quickly drafted to Nairobi Airport, where we were to board Comet 1 jet airliners. I thought: 'Hang on a minute, were these not the same aeroplanes that kept falling out of the skies'. When I raised this it was confirmed that there had been a problem, but it was because they were flying the aircraft too high, whereas our chances were good because we would cruising at thirty five thousand feet, a much safer height. Oh well that put my mind at rest, I think! The journey to the gulf only took four hours, and we certainly travelled first class. But I could not shake the idea that we were being used to find out if was safe and suitable, before paying passengers were allowed on board again.

We arrived at our army base during the night and I have never before or since known heat like it. We used our accommodation just to store our equipment, and slept out in the open all the time I was there. Not only was it hot, but it was also very humid. I noticed that there were no overweight Fusiliers amongst those who had been stationed there for the same time that we had been in Kenya. The food was basic and one of the extras that would be frowned on today was that we had to take daily salt tablets to compensate for the loss through perspiration.

To prepare us for possible action we were sent up the Gulf Straights to train for using boats for a beach landing. This was carried out in excessive heat and there were a number of cases of men suffering from heat exhaustion. The only way they could be treated effectively was to give them drinks of warm water and keep them doused in sea water. I noticed that most of the men affected were those who had come from Kenya. We just did not have enough time to become acclimatised.

Previously, I mentioned the guys from St Lucia. There were brothers named Edward and Cyprian, and a third fella called Lybird. During our time in the Gulf they decided to make three steel drums, one for the each of them. I asked Edward how he was going to tune them and he said it would be by ear. "I said: "Are you sure Ed?" He replied: "Yes trust me".

It was fortunate that the trouble in Bahrein was defused before it turned into full blown war, so we were glad to be informed that we would be posted back to Kenya. When we got back to Kenya, Eddy asked me to strike the keys of the NAAFI piano which corresponded to those of the steel drums and sure enough, every note played was pitch perfect. "Eddy", I said: "I am well impressed".

On arriving at the airport we were confronted not by a Comet 1 jet, but by a veteran wartime Dakota which carried stores and sometimes, like today, passengers. I just hoped the seats had been securely secured otherwise we were in for a bumpy ride. Fortunately they were and off we went. I was looking out of my square window when I noticed that the wing was flipping up and down slightly. I pointed this out to my mate Rod who was sitting next me, and he said he thought they always did that. "Really" I said, looking out of the opposite window onto the other wing. "Well that one isn't". About two minutes later, the co-pilot came through and told us to prepare for landing. Through luck rather than judgment, I fear, we were flying over an RAF airfield which I believe was called Salala. Thankfully, we landed safely. It transpired that one of the main support bars in the wing had become loose, and the worst case scenario could have been that the wing snapped off the fuselage.

We stayed there for a few hours, and were informed that another aircraft would take us on our way. And lo and behold it was another Dakota. So again we boarded but with some trepidation as you might have guessed. We thought that this was the craft that would take us to Kenya, but no, his orders were to take us to ADEN. 'Oh no' I thought. McGregor country!

We stayed in transit, for nearly a week and during that time I nearly met my Waterloo. It happened like this. One night, a friend and I got a taxi into a nearby town. On arriving we went into a café and got talking to a couple of Danish seamen, who were looking for some female company. I explained their need to the waiter, who said he would see what he could do. About half an hour later a man arrived with two ladies of the night. The Danish fellas did not have much English so the bartering for the ladies' company was left to me. The price that was asked was far too high and much to the man's annoyance the two seamen shrugged their shoulders, got up and left. We continued to stay there drinking our coffee. Then, suddenly my mate said "Johnny, I think we are in trouble". The man whom we had been talking to was now joined by two others and they were looking and pointing at us. At the same time, the window roller blinds were being lowered and they were indicating to the owner to lock the entrance door. On seeing this we both got up and ran for the door. My mate got through but I was tripped up and did not get out. What followed was that I was badly beaten and lost consciousness. From what my mate told me, it was in this condition that I was finally thrown out onto the street. My mate pulled me out of the road and propped me up against a wall. There was quite a lot of blood from my nose, so he took off my shirt and used my vest to clean me up as best he could. I was in severe pain in both rib areas and in the nether region, obviously from being kicked there. After about half an hour I had recovered sufficiently to get into a taxi and we made it back to camp. The next morning on parade I was asked what had happened by the inspecting sergeant. I said "that I had fallen down some steps, but that I was alright". I could not go sick for a proper examination, because, as one of the squaddies who was based in Aden told us, the place that we had been in the previous night was known as the Crater area and was strictly out of bounds to all service personal. He also said that I was lucky to get away with just a beating, since a number of soldiers had been murdered there recently.

In just over a week when I was still very sore, we finally boarded a Beverly aircraft on our final part of the journey back to Kenya. The Beverly was like a double decker bus and was very slow and only flew at ten thousand feet, which meant we had a great view of the landscape below. Finally, and with gratitude, we landed back at Nairobi Airport. It had taken us four hours to get to the Gulf and nearly eight days to get back.

The Christmas of nineteen fifty nine came, and it was normal, at this time to reminisce and think of loved ones back home. We missed them all, but recognised that compared to our comrades still in Bahrein, we should thank our lucky stars that we didn't have it too bad.

By now, our Corps of Drums was very slick, and every Saturday we would combine with the Regimental band and march up and down our football pitch to wonderful military marching music. I really did enjoy both the marching and the music. Although we had a proper football pitch we could only play for twenty minutes each way because of the high altitude we were at. However, when we went to Mombasa, on the coast, for leave, we all noticed how very much fitter we had become. So it came as no surprise to me in later life, when I was running marathons, that it was always the Kenyans who lived at high altitudes, who ran away with the honours.

On one particular morning Drum Major Rose was in a foul mood. Nothing we did could please him. Now, Lybird our brother from St Lucia, whose turnout always boarded on the casual side, received a very loud and continuous barrage about his attire. Finally, he was asked: "Well what have you got to say for yourself? Lybird answered in his beautiful patois. "Well man, nutting I seem to do pleases you so, I ad enough". With that, he put his bugle and drum down and strolled off down the road. The Drum Major went ballistic, screaming out to Lybird get back here "NOW". Without turning round, Lybird gave a casual, dismissive wave of his hand and replied: "No man, you ain't listening. I'm finished, do what you gotta do". He was finally found lying on his bed casually smoking a cigarette. Well, the Drum Major did do what he had to do, and this was to have two regimental policemen escort our fellow drummer to the guardhouse. He received fourteen days confined to barracks, but secretly became our hero, because what he did, especially as a national serviceman, many of us wished we had the same courage to do something similar. But what we did was to keep our traps shut and just take on the chin.

At the time I did not fully appreciate my time in Kenya, but on reflection I wished I had, because it is a wonderful and beautiful country. To put it into financial terms, if I had to pay at present for just a slight improvement regarding the accommodation and food that we enjoyed, it would cost thousands of pounds.

If you had spoken to the vast majority of conscripts, the one thing on their mind was the demob date, thus making the two years go very slowly. After nearly a year in total, we again travelled to Mombasa by train. On arriving there we boarded the Dunera for a second time and it took us to Malta, where the whole Battalion came together, and we relished meeting up with old pals again.

The St Andrews barracks in Malta, where we were now billeted were almost Victorian in design. Normally, we were three or four to a room, the ceilings were high, the floors consisted of marble black and white tiles and at the windows there were wooden slatted blinds. All in all it was a very nice improvement on what we were used to, especially the fellas from Bahrein. I arrived there with only four months of my service to do, and made a firm resolution to knuckle down and behave myself, and in the main I succeeded. However, at times there were marginal errors of judgement. For instance, Salima was nearby, a town where most of our Regiment and members of the, Navy and Marines would all go for a night out. Inevitably, on some occasions there were altercations. One night I went out with my mate Jimmy who was from the Engineers Regiment and others for a night out in a popular seafront pub. Jimmy was his regiment's boxing champion but coupled with this had a fine singing voice. Anyway we all went to pub prepared for a good night out, and on arriving there we found that it was filled with a good cross section of Her Majesty's forces. After getting a round of drinks in, Jimmy spoke to the pianist asking if he could sing a couple of songs. This was agreed. Jimmy went to the front of the stage and before starting to sing, he spoke into the mike and, attempting to call a truce, said: "Good evening lads. Just going to give you a couple of numbers, but before I do, wouldn't it be nice if, just for once we could have a good night out without any trouble". The response had a suspect air about it. But Jimmy gave a nod to the pianist, and in very good voice began to sing a popular song of the period. On the table in front of the stage, was a bearded burly sailor, who began making cat noises. Jimmy stopped singing and said: "Leave off mate, give us a chance". The sailor said: "I was just showing you that I am a better singer." Jimmy turned round and indicated for the pianist to start playing again. But as soon as he started the rest of the sailors around the table joined in the cat chorus. Jimmy slowly put down the microphone, got down from the stage, grabbed the sailor by his beard with his left hand and landed a right handed punch on the nose. With that, the bar erupted. Tables and chairs as well as fists were used as weapons. One of my mates, who had watched too many wrestling matches, tried a drop kick from the stage. Unfortunately his target sidestepped and he went sailing out of the entrance door into the arms of a Red Cap military policeman; so that was him out of the frame. Because this was an area where this kind of thing happened fairly regularly, the Shore Patrol, of the Navy and Marines as well as the Red Caps, were always on standby in the vicinity. They all charged, together, but at the same, all of us in the bar were in full retreat out of another entrance. It was not unusual, however, to see a hurt soldier being helped by a matelot or marine or vice versa, the reason being that by now, we all had a common enemy - the police in one form or another, who were collectively trying to bang us up.

I knew Malta quite well from my time in the Merchant Navy and one of my old haunts was a bar in a street in Valetta known as the Gut. One night I decided to make a return to this bar. On entering I was recognised immediately by the boss and his bar staff and was made very welcome. I was in there one night when two of my Maltese friends, whom I had known from Aldgate, in London, came in. Aldgate at that time had quite a few Maltese people living there and my two friends had a somewhat questionable reputation. On seeing me they both came rushing over, shaking me by the hand and throwing in a hug or two for good measure, and we had a really good night together. When they left the boss of the bar came over and said: "How do you know these two men"? I explained, I used to use a club they owned in East London. I don't know what kind of reputation they had in Malta, all I know is that I was treated very respectively from then onwards, and I hasten to say unjustifiably so.

I was on duty at the Barracks one night and at ten o' clock it was my role to play the Last Post, once again. At the same time the flag was lowered. Behind me, in formation, were the guard for the night and the men who were serving detention. In total, about twenty people. The officer in charge was standing on the brow of a hill which sloped sharply behind him, but unbeknown to either the officer or me was another mate of mine called

Ronnie, from the Royal Engineers regiment. He was concealed behind a small concrete structure. As I began to sound the call he stood up in full view of me and the men behind, and lobbed a big lump of mud and ducked down again out of site. The missile struck me on the leg, causing me to fluff a note. The guard and prisoners who witnessed this burst out laughing. The officer asked what was going on and I feigned ignorance. He told me to carry on and concentrate on my playing, but as soon I started, Ronnie lobbed another lump of mud and this time it struck me on the cheek. By this time the men behind were roaring with laughter. The officer looked round in all directions, but of course Ron had once again concealed himself. OK Drummer, let's give it one more try. So I did, and as soon as I sounded the first note, Ron stood up, but this time the officer spun round and saw him. "Stay exactly where you are man" said the Officer. "No chance": said Ron and legged it towards the coast exit road. The officer ordered the guard to go after him and fetch him straight back=, so they set off , more in lute warm rather than hot pursuit, so Ron made a clean get away. The officer asked where he was on the guards' return and they apologised saying that he was too fast for them. "Oh well", said the officer: "He won't get far. I will recognise him immediately". Of course, he was thinking that Ron was a member of our regiment.

On the battalions return from Kenya and Bahrein to Malta, we became linked with the 42 Commando Brigade. Not long after our arrival we were informed about a joint exercise. This time our destination was Libya, for desert training, which was ironic remembering half our regiment had just returned from Bahrein and as such were seasoned veterans of the sand.

During our stay in Libya, we visited a fourth century Roman site called Leptis Magna, which was wonderfully preserved. What struck me the most was that here we were as present day soldiers walking along the same road that Roman legionnaires had walked some sixteen hundred years ago. On returning to our accommodation we were confronted by a young boy who had a small box of coins which he said he had found on the site, and he asked if we would we like to buy any of them. It turned out that only one of us had any money, and he offered ten shillings for one of the coins, which the young boy agreed was an acceptable payment. When the fella who had bought the coin went home to the UK on leave, he made a visit to the Victoria and Albert Museum in London. He spoke to one of the curators regarding the value of the coin, and was told that it was in very good condition, and was pretty rare and on a good day might fetch two hundred and fifty pounds. Bloody hell the kid had a box full of them!

After nearly twenty months away, I went home on leave some two stones heavier. During my time served, I had quit smoking which of course increased my appetite and my fitness level was also pretty good. There was now another problem: the uniform that my girlfriend Brenda had so carefully tailored was a tad too small. Not an issue, I thought. Just don't breathe out too much.

By now my family had moved from Jersey Road, to a brand new flat in West Ham. To my Mum and Dad this was like five star accommodation in comparison to what they had been used to. At last I knocked on the door of Nineteen Holland Road, and it was opened by both parents. "Good to have you home son" they said. "And it's dammed good to be here" I replied. My leave came and went far too quickly and so back to Malta to complete my time in the army.

I was on my last duty as a bugle playing soldier, and was sitting outside the guardroom in between calls. I saw the Regimental Sergeant Major heading in my direction, and on nearing me he said "I understand you are going back to the Tower tomorrow for demob? I stood up to attention and replied: "That's right Sir". Then he said "Just as I was passing I noticed your hair was a bit long, I suggest you have a haircut, and when you have, report back to me". So I did just that, just a nice little trim, and reported back to the RSM as ordered. He said: "Take your beret off and let's have a look". I complied with his request. He enquired: "Ringwood, do you know the rules about haircuts?" "Not really sir" I replied. He said, "Well, it goes like this. All that is under your beret is yours and all that is on the outside is mine, do you understand?" "Fully" I replied. So back to the barbers I went. Just to refresh readers' memories, during my initial training I purchased a tiny Belgian beret and this was the one I was now wearing. On entering the barbers I pulled the beret down as far as I could, but it still looked like a pimple on a haystack. I told the barber to cut my hair to just under the rim. It looked ridiculous. You have to remember this this was Malta and I had a very good tan, except for the big white blob on the back of my head. I once again returned to the RSM who with a little smile said: "Ah that's what I call a haircut. Dismiss!"

So, with just two days to go, just as it was in the beginning when I tried to pull a few strokes, the army had the last say.

Seventeen: Brenda

Although I didn't appreciate it at the time, one of the most important occasions of my life was when I met Brenda. It was at a party in a house in Varley Road, just two turnings from Jersey Road. She was just the kind of girl I needed; hardworking, straight as a die, and loyal. With Brenda, what you see is what you get. On coming out of the army she was ready to pick up where we had started nearly two years ago. I remember saying to her "I haven't got a lot mate, but I promise you we will never want for anything. What about getting married? So, in her normal off the cuff way, she answered: "Ok why not, let's give it a go". Sure enough, a few weeks later at West Ham Registrar's Office we tied the knot. There was just a small gathering of close friends and relations. We held our reception party at the Gun Pub on the Isle of Dogs, we used an upper room where Lord Nelson is supposed to have had his rendezvous with Lady Hamilton. I reckoned, if it was good enough for him, it was good enough for us. We were well looked after by the host, because the Gun was my Dad's regular drinking hole, and he was also the resident singer. We went back there for our fiftieth anniversary, but now it is a very classy eating venue as well as a pub. After the meal I ventured upstairs to the upper room where we had held our reception. I opened the door only to find that it was being used for a woman's fortieth birthday party. I apologised immediately, but the woman asked me if I was from the fiftieth anniversary celebration. I said that I was and said again that I regretted the intrusion, but went on to explain that this was the room where we had held our wedding reception. The lady said that she and her guests were all new to the area, and that if I had got a minute, could I please tell them what it was like around here fifty years ago. But before starting she invited me to have a glass of champagne with them, and for the next ten minutes I did just that. She thanked me and said that it would be nice to meet my wife. I said that I wouldn't promise anything but I would give it a try. Now, unlike me Brenda likes to keep a low profile. So, with this mind I re-joined our party. Brenda asked where I had been. I said I had been upstairs in our old reception room, but did not tell her about the celebration being held there. "Would you like to have a look?" I asked. She replied: "Yes, that would be nice". We went up to the room and I opened the door. Immediately everyone there stood up and clapped. Brenda looked at me with a look that said you SOD, and the lady gave Brenda a glass of bubbly and a beautiful bouquet of flowers saying: "Here you are my dear you deserve them more than me". What a wonderful gesture, one which I am sure Lord Nelson would have approved of.

Eighteen:
Back to reality

It really did not take me to long to get back into the swing of things, and the first task was to get a job. Sitting round the dinner table my Dad asked if I wanted to go back to sea. I replied that I might do that in the future but not yet, and that I was thinking about going back into ship repairing. I asked him what he thought about that. He said: "Well you were known as a grafter and a strong kid in the past and now, coupled with that extra weight and muscle, getting the work should not be a problem". Sure enough, the next day, in his place of work which was still Rye Arc he asked the Governor if there was a place for me. He agreed readily, so once again, it was back to the Monday hammer.

Nineteen:
Our first two sons

It was not unusual for newlyweds to stay with their parents, and that is what happened to Brenda and me. For the first year it was with my Mum and Dad and for the next three it was with Brenda's parents. It was whilst living at my Mum and Dad's flat, that our first son Terry was born, and I became one proud dad. The first thing I did was to buy a large Silver Cross pram. It was navy blue and white and there were two large wheels at the rear and two smaller at the front, all with a high chrome finish. I looked after that pram like it was a Rolls Royce, and when I was pushing it down the Barking Road in Canning Town, with my boy inside, I felt like I was on top on the world. Three years' later, when living at Brenda's parents we were once again blessed with another fine boy, whom we named Stephen.

Twenty:
Dark Times

My work in the dock was not as regular as I needed it to be, so I decided that I would return to the Merchant Navy. I discussed this with Brenda, who was not too keen on the idea, but agreed we needed a regular income. So, along to the Shipping Federation I went, to see what my chances were. There wasn't a problem as long as I still had my steward's kit and uniform, which I did. I learned there was a job going on the Gothic, which was the ship I had sailed on just prior to going into the army. Once again, I joined her and set sail for New Zealand, but as soon as we were going down the English Channel I regretted it. Coupled with this I was not feeling my normal chirpy self. In fact it was the opposite: I was beginning to feel really depressed and was also having what I now know to be panic attacks. There seemed to be no reason for this. Here I was happily married with a fine little son, doing a job which I had previously loved, so what was going on? I did not seek any medical help, because I considered I could work it out for myself, and really tried to give no outward signs to anyone of the torment I was going through. The four months that the trip lasted was something I never wanted to endure again. If I had been at home, at least I could have shared my anxieties with Brenda who has always been a fountain of strength. I never, ever told her in my letters of my problems since I did not want to worry her. Finally, we arrived back in the Royal Docks, I got discharged and home I went. On arriving, Brenda immediately knew something was radically wrong. I had lost a lot of weight and was looking pretty haggard. Next day she insisted that I attend our local surgery. On speaking to the doctor and explaining what had happened, his response shook me to the core. He told me that I was having a mental breakdown and that I needed help. He said that he would be sending me to St Clements Hospital in Mile End where they would be able to help me. I asked when that would happen and he said it would be as soon as a place becomes available, which turned out to be within a week.

St Clements was a real eye opener. The first thing that happened was that I was prescribed Valium. Later I discovered was highly addictive, and because I was on a very high dosage to start with, the side effects were not unpleasant: I loved everybody. We were given woodwork to do and I made a very nice bedside cabinet. Then there was group therapy, which really helped because suddenly, I was listening to other people who had almost exactly similar problems to me. It indicated that I wasn't as mad as I thought I was when my doctor said initially that had suffered a mental breakdown. But I was ill and so were they. It helped to talk about it but it did not seem to help relieve my depression or panic attacks. These attacks would become more severe if, for instance, I was on the underground trains. I would always stand in the corner facing the side of the train, so that the other passengers would not see me sweating buckets. At the most I would last only two stations before I had to get off. This disabling effect went on for two years, and I overcome the problem finally, by travelling on the trains late at night and gradually increasing the number of stations before getting off, until at last I got over it. On one occasion I was having a consultation with a female psychiatrist when she asked me how I felt. I replied: "Edgy, just like a square with all the corners jutting out, not being able to relax". Then she asked how I would like to feel and I replied: "Like a ball just rolling along and going with the flow". She said she liked that response and would use it as an illustration in the future.

Recently, I have read that regular exercise helps to counter depression, and some fifty five years ago, this was also my way of lessening its effects. My logic was that after a good session in the gym or running a few miles on the road, I always felt good, so it seemed common sense to keep the body fit, because the more you exercised the more the body created the 'feel good' endorphins. In drawing this painful episode to a close, I need to say that when I read of some very famous people going through the same sort of ordeal and surviving well, in a strange way it helped. I think of Winston Churchill, especially, who called his depressive episodes his Black Dog, which seems very apt. My advice is to stick with it because when you finally get out of the bottom of that well, and you will do so, you will be a far stronger person both mentally and physically than you were before. Just adopt a positive attitude.

Twenty-One:
The Manor Road Buildings

With two sons in the fold, we qualified for accommodation from the council, but not however without the normal hassle. Finally, we were given a flat in the Manor Road buildings, which at that time did not have a very good reputation. Our place was on the third floor, so humping the big pram up and down certainly enhanced my fitness levels. On moving into our three bedroom flat, I was very pleasantly surprised. Our main source of heat was once again just one fire in the living room, on which according to today's values, we burned far too much coal. It was well over two hundredweight a week, but I am afraid my priority was to ensure that my family would never experience the cold, as I had in my childhood. Within a few months, because of my background in the Merchant Navy and the Army, the flat shone like a new pin. I was earning good money in the docks so I was able to decorate and furnish it to a pretty good standard.

The stairs and landings were communal which meant we each had our own landing and stairs to keep clean. I was determined to try and maintain a good standard throughout the block and set about this by having a talk with rest of the residents on how collectively, we could achieve this, and it was agreed, with the exception of one tenant. Because I was not going to let this one tenant spoil our intentions, I took it on to clean her areas as well. It was great to hear the delivery people comment that this was the cleanest block in the buildings. The fly-in-the-ointment tenant lived directly below us, and it was clear, right from the beginning of our tenancy, that she had mental health problems. Almost immediately after moving in, she would bang on the ceiling with a broom handle, the first time this happened I went down and knocked on her door and asked what the problem was. She replied that she wanted us to stop dancing around on the floorboards which was causing all her lights to shake. I replied: "Lady, all my floors are carpeted and secondly, all we were doing when you started to bang, was sitting down watching the television". This kind of disturbance went on week after week, until I said to Brenda: "That's it. If she wants noise, I will give her some". So again, just as we were preparing to put the boys to bed she started banging with her broom handle for a good twenty seconds. At this, I stood the boys on the back of the settee and told them to jump down, and we repeated this at least ten times. However, all it did was to escalate the problem, because her next performance was like a drum roll. But I think I found her Achilles heel on the next occasion. This happened at about eleven pm, and I was just dropping off to sleep, when she began. I let her finish, then asked Brenda if I could borrow one of her high heeled shoes. I used it to bang on the floor once every five seconds. I persevered until I heard her scream out that she was going to get the police, so I stopped and went to sleep. The following week I took the family away for a week's holiday.

Whilst we were away, our beloved neighbour went and complained that she had had no sleep for a week because of the noise from us. When asked about the timing of this, she replied that it had been happening all week. On returning home, we were confronted by an officer from the council and were told that if we continued to harass the tenant below us then we could face eviction. I asked when this alleged disturbance had occurred and he answered that according to the complainant it had been all of last week. I answered: "That is very strange my friend, because, we were away all last week on holiday, and here are the snapshots to prove it". Then I explained that in realty, the shoe was on the other foot, and that we were the ones that had suffered her continuous banging on her ceiling with no rhyme or reason. He apologised and said he would look into the matter further.

It all came to a head about a week later. We had just put the boys to bed when the son of the neighbour in question started to play his record player so loud that it woke the boys up, causing Steve to cry. I said to Brenda: "That's it mate, I have had enough". I went down and knocked on their flat door, which was opened by the son who said: "What the f*****g hell do you want?" I replied: "Do me a favour and turn your music down a bit please". He replied with some more dismissive abuse, and his mother joined in adding her insults. The punch that landed on his chin was packed with months of torment. On his way down I got him in a neck lock and continued to pound his face. His mother was now on my back screaming for me to stop. When I had vented my feelings enough I let him fall, and both he and I were covered in blood. By now, all the rest of the tenants in the block were on the scene, and one of them said: "We wondered when you were going to do something like that" . I said that they had stepped over the line this time in upsetting my children. Brenda cleaned me up and I changed my clothes, knowing what was to follow, and sure enough, in just a few minutes, two policemen were knocking on my door. "Come in officers" I said.

One of them said: "Okay mate. Your neighbour wants us to charge you with assault and battery, and from what we have seen of him he just may have a case. So what have you got to say for yourself?" I replied at length, explaining the amount of prolonged provocation we had suffered, unjustifiably, in every way. A couple of my other neighbours, who were in the kitchen keeping an eye on Brenda, who was in a bit of a state, heard what I was saying. Rightly or wrongly, the man came into the living room and said to both of the policemen. "If Johnny wants any witnesses to act in his defence we will be queuing up to do it". The officer then said to our neighbour: "Thanks for that, we will keep it in mind". He then said that I may have to come to the police station, but that first he had to speak to the neighbours downstairs to get their version of the event. They returned about an hour later, and by then I was ready to go with them. The first officer said: "Relax, you are not going anywhere". I asked what made them change their minds and he replied "that it was very clear, even to a layman that there were signs that the woman was mentally unstable". Also, what really swung it in my favour were the hundreds of indentations in the ceilings, in every room made by the worn top of a broom handle. He said that he had told the son that although he may have a case for assault, in the main he had provoked me enough to goad me into losing control. In addition, if he wished to proceed any further, they would have to report, to the council, the wilful damage that he and his mother had done to the ceilings of their flat also the nuisance problems they had created, which in turn could lead to their eviction. "So how do wish to go forward?" the officer had asked. The son had replied "If that's the case I had better drop it". Nevertheless, the council must have got wind of the problem, because just a few weeks later, the family was rehoused to a different area. So, at last the whole block now was on an even keel.

After six years in the Manor Road Buildings, my youngest son Michael was born at home. My wife was in the spare bedroom awaiting the birth, and in attendance with her was a young Chinese trainee nurse waiting for the Midwife to come. I was in the living room serenading my other two boys with my guitar, when suddenly there was a cry from the young trainee, saying "Mr Ringwood you come quickly, baby coming now". So, in I rushed without having a clue what to do, but we had prepared the room in accordance with the midwife's guidance, and all I had to do was to fetch a bowl of warm water. After a very short time Michael was born and as I saw him take his first breath, I swear on the second one he asked me to lend him a fiver. Now we had three sons, and my pride had increased accordingly.

My Mum little Win

My handsome Dad

My ever patient wife Brenda keeping a tight rein on me.

My wife Brenda and our three sons Michael, Steve and Terry.

My Grand children first photo taken 2001 second 2016, wonderful Christmas present.

End of the war Jersey Road street party, Mum holding my sister Irene back row, brother Jimmy second left front row, at this time I was at Fyfield fattening up school.

First class steward 1955

Corps of Drums Malta 1959, doing my bit far right front row.

Signing in in the reception office of Kings College Cambridge 1965, Im'e the one with the ironed hair.

Celebrating with a glass of Champagne at the installation of The Docker Statue, with Les Johnson in the straw hat, yours truly on the middle and the boys from the foundry Royal Victoria Dock London 2009.

Twenty-Two:
West Ham Power Station

After working in the dock for some time, I thought a change of job was due. It so happened, that one of my neighbours told me that they were looking to hire people at West Ham Power Station, which was very close to the Manor Road Buildings. I applied and was told to come for an interview, so along I went. The man carrying out the interview asked what my previous job was and I replied that I had been a fitter's mate, working on marine engines in the docks. He said that was very fortunate for me because they had been looking for someone like me to be a mate for one of their engineering fitters, whose job it was to maintain their turbines. Then he asked me if I was very strong, because at times the work is very heavy, I would be expected to swing a fourteen pound hammer for lengthy periods. He said: "Do you think you can handle that"? With a wry smile I replied: "I think so sir". I worked there for eleven years, progressing through the ranks until I became a Turbine Operator.

It was one of the best jobs I have ever had. It was shift work which meant one week you would work three twelve hour night shifts, and the following week it would be four twelve hour day shifts. By that time, West Ham power station was getting towards its sell by date so on many of the night time shifts, it would not be needed by the national grid. Therefore it became very common practice to get your head down for the night, especially if we had arranged to go fishing the next day. To make myself comfortable during one of these night of shifts, I purchased a camp bed that had metal spring struts that fitted underneath. So with the bed tucked neatly under my duffel coat I went into the gate house to clock in. But on doing so, I forgot about the bed and it came crashing down onto the tiled floor, in front of everybody, including my foreman. He called me over to one side and said: "Johnny boy we all know what goes on, but for Gawd sake don't rub my bleeding nose in it. Now pick up thy bed and walk". Good man, great job!

As already stated, holidays even in the early sixties, were not taken for granted, so by way of compensation, days out to the seaside, commonly known as Beanos were an annual event from streets, pubs and places of work. The resort we chose for the Power station outing was Margate. Before leaving, we called into the nearby pub called the Bridge House, and were there for about an hour, getting well lubricated. Although it was high summer we all wore suits and ties, but we did splash out and buy straw hats. On arriving at Margate we all went into the nearest watering hole, and continued wearing our whistle and flutes (suits), but by now, one of our colleagues, Fred, had had too much booze and all he wanted to do was to get his head down and have a kip. So I took him onto the beach put his jacket on back to front, to stop him getting sunburnt, and laid him next to a jellied eel stall. However, the female proprietor said you can't leave him there: when the tide comes in he will be drowned. Besides, he is not a very good advert! By then, he was out of it, so I shifted him onto a nearby bench. But before doing so, I took a photo of him. The following week I showed Fred the developed photo. He wasn't best amused, because Fred was old school, a gentleman and easily embarrassed. He said: "Johnny, have you shown this to anyone else"? I replied: "Of course not mate. It was just for your eyes, as a reminder of the good time you had". He said: "Can I keep it John, along with any negatives you may have, as a reminder that there's no fool like an old fool".

One day whilst at work, I was approached by one of the managers who asked me to accompany him to the Superintendent's office. On arriving he asked me to sit down, then said: "I'm not sure if you are aware of this, but each Power Station in the country, has been asked to send a representative to a week's seminar, to be held at Kings College, Cambridge". I said that I had not heard about it, but if chosen would be delighted to attend. Also I wondered why I had been picked to go. He responded by saying that I was the youngest employee at the station and that management were impressed by the way you had conducted yourself since my employment began there. Lastly he said that they thought I would do them proud.

The day came for me to attend and on arriving at Kings College, it was all a bit surreal. What was this young tyke from Custom House doing in what is one of the most famous universities in the world? But it got even better. Our accommodation was in the same rooms used by the students (who were on leave for half term). Our meals were served in their beautiful dining room, and our seminars were held in the same lecture rooms that they used.

Whilst there we were allowed into the wonderful Kings College Chapel, and were very fortunate to sit and listen to the world famous choir rehearse: a truly wonderful experience.

At the end of the week we had a farewell dinner and concert, and the cast of the concert was drawn from course members. My contribution was a couple of Frank Sinatra numbers which seem to go down well. At the end of the evening the Principal gave a speech, in which he jokingly indicated that we could now be called King's Men. I put my hand up and asked if it was alright to wear the old school tie. He replied that he thought I would have to attend a little bit more than a week for me to be granted that request. On my return to work I went and thanked the Superintendent for a wonderful, memory making week.

Twenty-Three:
Into the light

I was never quite sure why our Buildings had such a poor reputation. Sure there were some tenants who were a bit rough around the edges, but that could be said for any street or road in Newham. No, on the whole our six years spent there were fine. At the rear of our block and the block behind was a large communal area that contained our coal sheds and open spaces for clothes drying, and each landing had a balcony that overlooked these spaces. Our children also used these spaces as playgrounds, which gave us all peace of mind because there was no traffic to worry about.

We were the first Tenants' Association to be formed in the Borough. I was approached by its chairman, a fella called Bob who asked if I would be interested in joining: this I readily agreed to. I liked Bob straight away. He was a typical East Ender; witty, sharp and someone who knew his way around the block. I attended a few meetings of the Association at which most of the business seemed to comprise discussion of plans and action for cutting through the reams of red tape created by the council. But eventually we started to get results.

One day Bob invited me round to his place for a get together that evening. We agreed that I would pop in at about 7 o'clock for 'a cup of tea'. So round to his place I went and knocked on the door, which was opened by Bob, and he invited me in. I followed him into the living room, which was fairly crowded with men and woman praying and praising God. I quickly became a black smith and made a bolt for the door and legged it home. On arriving, Brenda remarked that that was a very quick cup of tea, so I explained what had gone on. A couple of days went by and I bumped into Bob in the street. I asked him what all that was about round at his place the other night. He replied that perhaps he should have told me they were all Christians, but said that, as we were standing in the middle of the pavement, we could not talk there. He asked if I had half an hour to spare. I said that of course I had, and he suggested we go over to the recreation ground where he would explain where he was coming from, which he did at length. As he was talking it wasn't like listening to a vicar. This was someone from my neck of the woods. "Well, what do you think?" He asked. "Nah, that's not for me Bob." I said. " Alright mate. He said. "But, do go away and think about it, and I have got to tell you that I am going to pray for you". Of course, I was putting up a front, because my mind kept going back to that time when I was sitting alone on the deck of that boat in the middle of the Indian Ocean, with the night sky covered by what seemed millions of stars. I knew then that there was a power that was far more mighty and powerful than man.

However, I wasn't going to give in that easily: no way. There were a lot of questions that needed answering, so I started to put them to Bob, and to be fair to him he did fairly well. "John he said the people you met round my place are called a home group, but we all belong to the Mayflower Church, the Warden of which is the Rev David Sheppard; and if that names rings a bell, not long ago he was the England Cricket Captain. Do you want to come along and meet him?" I replied: "why not; it will be an honour? "

So on the following Sunday I went along to the Mayflower, sat through the service and met the great man along with his lovely wife Grace. He was not only a great cricketer, but also a very powerful preacher. But equally, he was a man's man who commanded respect. On the third week of attendance, Skipper (that is what we called him) asked me if I would like to join his Searchers Group. This was formed for people like me, who were looking for answers. I attended that group every week for seven months, asking every conceivable question that I could think of. Until finally, one night, he said: "Johnny you have emptied my theological barrel, I have no more answers, so now it is my turn. Do believe that the Bible is the word of the Lord?" I answered: "Yes". "Do you believe that Jesus is the son of God?" I replied that I did. "Do you believe that to enter into the faith you must seek forgiveness?" "I do". I replied. "Then go home, get onto your knees and ask the Lord to rule and reign in your life. Because our belief is based on faith, only by accepting his grace will you experience this gift".

That is exactly what I did. I knelt down on my knees in my bathroom, with the door locked because I did not want to be disturbed. My prayer went something like this: Lord I have done many things in my life that I am not very proud of, but during the last few months I have been informed that you will forgive my sins. If I pray that you will come into my life to be my Lord and saviour. I am not sure of the right words to say, but this is what I pray will happen. If I am accepted into your kingdom, then I promise you that I will try to change my ways to become more like the good Christians who I have met over the last few months, especially Bob and Skipper. I find it difficult to put onto paper what happened next, but I will try. In the bible after Jesus was crucified, he appeared to some of his disciples and told them that he was going back to heaven, but he would be sending a replacement. This replacement was the Holy Spirit. I did not get any flames from heaven or anything like that. But for the next three months I experienced that same sense of peace and joy that I had on that night in the Indian Ocean.

Now I want you to remember, that it's not so long ago that I had suffered a nervous breakdown and so marked was the difference in my behaviour that my wife thought it was time to send for the men in the white coats. I tried to explain what was happening but I really didn't know myself. I wasn't versed enough in the scriptures to understand how much I was being blessed. I have spoken to many Christians over the years about this and nearly all of them said that it didn't happen to them. The only conclusion I can come to is that those three months were a Holy term of reference, so that when my faith starts to weaken, as it has on occasions, I hear the words very clearly. "Leave off Johnny boy. I was with you in the Spirit for three solid months. How much more proof do you want?"

I gave my life to Christ in June nineteen sixty seven, I am writing this in two thousand and seventeen, and that is a pretty long time. Through his grace I have achieved many things that without him in my corner, would have been impossible. One man said to me: "You only went into religion because you had a need". He was referring to my breakdown. I replied: "Yes fair enough. So would you not turn to your father if you were in trouble? Because that's what I did except it was my heavenly father, and he gave me far more than healing. I also received his guidance, through his son the Lord Jesus's teaching". But there was a problem: he also gave me a conscience that is as big as 'St Pauls Cathedral'.

I worshipped at the Mayflower for over thirty years and met many wonderful Christians, but the most impressionable memories to stay with me, were the sacrifices made by the people who came to lead at the Mayflower over that time, when they came to Canning Town, not only to work but also to live

As already explained, David Sheppard was the English cricket captain, and if he had chosen another route I am sure that he would have been a rich and highly thought of business man. His lovely wife Grace had a couple of pretty rough years when they first arrived, but they continued to live, lead and worship there for over eleven years. David, in his last post was the Bishop of Liverpool, and finally was made a Lord. After he had died I went to his Remembrance Service, in Liverpool Cathedral, which was packed to the rafters. Later, when I spoke to Lady Grace, she said: "You know, Johnny we could have filled this place twice with the people who wanted to pay their respects." I replied: "I'm not surprised: he was a great man."

David's Curate was Brian Seaman and together they made a great team. Brian and his wife Marion also made their home locally. Brian visited me when I was in hospital during the time that I was pretty low in spirits. I really appreciated those visits.

Following Skipper and Brian was Roger Sainsbury, who later became the Bishop of Barking. Roger was accompanied by his wife Jenny, again people with no links to the area or the locals, who initially, might have felt very much out of their comfort zone.

Roy Trevivian was another recruit to the work at the Mayflower. Roy's post prior to that was Head of religious broadcasts for the BBC. The radio station which preceded Radio 1 was called the Light Programme, and Roy had a daily God spot on it at five to nine in the morning. He was known as one of the most influential speakers in his field, but he fell out with his bosses for whatever reasons. So, he left the BBC and applied for a position at the Mayflower which had become vacant.

Roy had a history of depression and was also known to have a bit of a drink problem. Roger gave me this information and asked for my opinion about giving him the post of Curate. I replied: "If he is willing give up his present position to come to us in Canning Town let's give him a chance." In addition, my logic took into account the fact that in the area within the influence of the Mayflower there are many people who also suffer from depression and have an alcohol problem, and who better to minister to them than someone who is afflicted by the same demons. Thus, Roy was appointed. He never let us down and proved to be a committed and valuable member of the Mayflower family. Also, he became one of my closest and fondest friends.

I am writing this chapter in Easter week, and I am reminded of the event that we carried out on one particular Good Friday. Roger and Roy decided that if you want to get across the message of the trial and crucifixion of Jesus, then the best way was to bring it to the public attention in a place where there would be a lot of local people in attendance. We decided on Rathbone Market, a typical East End open air marketplace, which was always packed on Good Friday. A flat backed, open lorry was the stage. On it sat Roger, as Pontius Pilate the Roman Governor, dressed in appropriate clothing for the period. His character's task on the day was to Judge Jesus, who was accused of blasphemy, and Roy's role, along with other members of the Mayflower was to heckle and condemn.

My role was that of a Roman Legionary. My attire was a helmet, toga, a short leather skirt and sandals, and since this was a day in March, the skirt did not help very much, to allay the cold in the nether regions. My task as the legionary was to lead Jesus who was carrying a large wooden cross, through the market. I created a passageway through the crowds by calling out in my best imperious voice: "Make Way! Make Way!" The startled looks we received as we followed the path through is something that will stick in my mind for ever.

Jesus was played by one of our youth leaders, Geoff. He was a tall, thin man with long brown hair and a beard, so he did not need much make up to resemble popular interpretations of the appearance of the Lord. But the depiction of his trial and torture meant that Geoff's had been stained blood red, as if caused by the crown of thorns, that in his case was very carefully and gently placed on his head.

On arriving at the lorry the trial began. As history has told us Jesus was found guilty. The place where the 'crucifixion' was to take place was in the centre of a raised, grassed area, of what was then the Canning Town roundabout. So, with me leading the group, we set off, but this time there was a large following. A position for the cross had already been prepared and on arriving the cross was placed into it. Geoff was loosely tied to it, with his arms outstretched, but with his feet on the ground. He maintained this position for a good period of time, and as you can imagine there were a lot of double takes from passing motorists!

During their time at the Mayflower Roger and Roy had a vision for a youth club, which, in due time became a reality at the cost of over a million pounds. The money was provided by a tremendous fund raising effort, but for most of us it was supported by prayer and a sense of the Lord's approval.

Sadly, whilst he was with us, Roy suffered a terrible stroke, which robbed him of his speech. It was so was devastating to lose his oratory skills, and he would get terribly frustrated, because he thought that we could understand what he was trying to say.

When the right time arrived, we got together and found him a place at the famous Star and Garter Home for ill ex-service men. I used to visit him and was glad that he was so well looked after. Finally, went home to die in his beloved Cornwall. I had grown to love this man and missed him greatly.

The next couple who arrived to shepherd the flock at the Mayflower were a former Head Teacher, Edward Furness, and his lovely and gentle wife Sue. Now Sue was totally blind, so as well as having her lifestyle completely changed, she had to learn to cope, physically with her new surroundings.

Edward was later joined by Peter Watherstone, whose 'cut glass' accent immediately indicated that he was from the 'top draw'. If any further proof were needed his father was Sir David Watherstone K.B.E. Whilst at the Mayflower Peter met and fell in love with a miner's daughter from Doncaster.

Their wedding service was held at the Mayflower and the reception took place in the very large communal dining room. I have always loved the various accents and dialects that form the language of our country and I found it totally fascinating to hear the different accents from the two families, Peter and Hannah were two very special people who had at least one vital thing in common; their very deep faith, which appears to cuts through all so-called class boundaries.

On one special evening, Peter took me to dinner in the Goldsmiths' Hall in London where the annual Christmas celebration was being held. This was London at its best. As we entered, a choir assembled on the staircase, sung beautiful carol. As we were going into the main hall, Peter said: "Johnny, if you look up to the top of the stained glass window you will see the family crest". ' Wow! I thought to myself. That's class!'

Meanwhile, in the youth club, Pip Wilson, a tough scouser from Liverpool was appointed as youth leader. In my view, Liverpool has a lot in common with Canning Town, sharing a history of being dockland areas, and needing to undergo radical transformation. So, as far as I was concerned Pip totally knew the score. He was also a very devout Christian. Every night, he would have a God Spot, but because of his background the young local fellas did occasionally listen without giving him too much stick. The above is just a snapshot of the leadership at the Mayflower. There were many other people who shared my Christian journey there and I will never forget them.

Twenty-Four:
New Home

I decided to apply to the Council to find out whether it was possible to be rehoused. Subsequently a council officer called and said that as we had 'turned our flat into a little palace and we had been good tenants', he would approve our application. I think another factor might have been that, on many occasions, I had been a pain in the backside of the council in a number of disputes, whilst I was serving on the Tenants' Association, and they may have wanted me out of the way. Well, whatever the reason, we were rehoused in a lovely three bedroomed home, back in my beloved Custom House. This was one of the Lord's first blessings. We had a small front and back garden, which I soon got stuck into, and in no time there was a lawn and roses in the front and a pond and aviary at the back. As already mentioned, our home was at 25, Murray Square and the old communal spirit was in good flow. Very soon, we got to know most of our neighbours, many of whom had been rehoused from the old haunts such as Jersey Road. By now such roads had all been demolished. We knew they were a bit rough but the term given to this operation, 'slum clearance' tugged at the heart strings a bit.

Twenty-Five:
New start

By now, the life of West Ham Power Station really was coming to a close, so I took redundancy. I had made my mind up to try and get a trade under my belt and fortunately the government, at that time, were offering a six months' course on various trades, of which one was carpentry, and that was something I had always wanted to have a go at. The first obstacle I had to overcome was an English and mathematics test which was held at the local Labour Exchange. I had no problems with the English but I have always had a problem with maths, so it was no surprise when the lady in charge said that she was sorry, but that I had failed on the maths side. I shrugged and told her that I wasn't surprised, and was about to leave. The next thing that happened was to change my whole future life. The lady in question, Mrs Abercrombie asked me to sit down and said: "You are obviously an intelligent young man. Have you always had this problem with maths? I replied: "Yes I have a short retention thing regarding mathematics. I remember the equations for a short period then they go". Then she said: "Well, young man the questions are going to remain the same for the next two weeks. Do you think you can remember them and how to arrive at the answers, if someone points you in the right direction?". "I will certainly give it a try", I said. Now, one of my mates was a carpenter, so I contacted him and asked for some help. I explained that the questions involved decimals, fractions and division and these were to be used in measurements. So, for the next two weeks we got stuck into it. The day then came for the re-sit. I could not believe it when this wonderful lady told me: "Well done. You have passed. Not only that, you have achieved high marks". I have never forgotten Mrs Abercrombie, because if she had allowed me to leave without giving me another chance, my life would have been totally, and I mean totally, different. Angels come in different guises. I love her to bits. Over the years I would meet her in East Ham closed market, and she always enquired how I was doing? My answer was always the same. "Thanks to you Mrs Abercrombie, very well".

Twenty-Six:
Budding Carpenter

On the first day of the course there was another small test. I suppose it was to satisfy the facilitators and the Labour Exchange that they were singing from the same hymn book. Thankfully, I passed that one too. We were issued with a very good set of carpentry tools, and for the first few weeks, were taught the basic rudiments of working with wood. This was coupled with a lot of written English and maths homework. I took to it like a duck to water. I thought I had found my niche, until I got into the real world and discovered that as well as having some skill, speed was also a very highly valued factor, especially when your efforts and rewards are bonus related.

The six months seem to flash by, and after a final skills test, I was informed by the management, that I had reached the required standard to be sent to Tower Hamlets Maintenance department, as a trainee carpenter. So, with my box of tools, off I went. I have got to say that I wasn't very well received by some of the fully trained chippies, who in some cases had served a seven year apprenticeship, and in a way, I could see where they were coming from. But after a while they took me on board and showed me skills that you can only find when working in the real world. The job that we were carrying out was converting old blocks of flats into something more modern. It was really interesting but at times, also very dirty, especially when pulling up floor boards that had been in position since Victorian times.

As the months went by I was gaining skills and speed. Then, one day, after I had been on the job for about eighteen months, my foreman said: "Johnny I think you are ready to chance your arm as a chippy, but don't do with Tower Hamlets, go to Newham Council, where I have heard they are looking for maintenance carpenters". Following that advice, I sent off for an application form and was called for an interview. I was given a test consisting of repairing a door frame that had been smashed as if it had been burgled. In retrospect, this was a very valid test because I had to carry out this repair on number of occasions. I won't go into the technicalities of the job, except to say that if there are any chippies reading this they were looking to see if I could repair the frame with a scarf joint. I met the required standard and was given a job.

I thoroughly enjoyed the job because it was so varied. Sometimes, you were repairing old work and on other occasions you would be installing new structures. One job was to replace a balcony door in a flat that was seventeen floors up in a Tower Block. I was accompanied by Eric, my labourer. We knocked on the door and it was opened by an elderly man who invited us in to start the job. Almost as soon as I had opened my tool box to start work, the man started on about his budgie, which I had noticed sitting in his cage in the corner chirping away. The old boy said: "This is Joey, best talker this side of the Canning Town Bridge. You 've never heard nuffing like it, I'm telling Ya." Sure enough, his little vocabulary had phrases like: 'who's a pretty boy' and such like, but the old fella kept on and on trying to get the budgie to give us its full range. We had come to the point where we had to remove the old balcony door in order to replace it with the new one. We undid the final screw on the hinge, which enabled Eric to lift the door free, when suddenly, there was a flutter of wings, a flash of blue and out of the cage and through the door opening went Joey boy. "Shit!" said the old fella. "I forgot to lock his cage." I had thought he was out of earshot when I said to Eric "You would have thought, with all that chat he would have had the decency to say Goodbye!, a remark I think he did not appreciate! However, I did try to make amends by getting him another budgie.

Another time, Eric and I were putting new window frames in a block of flats ten storeys high. It was winter time and we were on the top floor working off a scaffold. The flat was occupied by a real old character who ran an egg stall in the nearby market place. He opened one of the newly installed windows a little and said: "Cold out there boys ain't it? "Freezing" I replied. With that he passed out two large measures of whisky. "Get that down yah. That'll warm the cockles of your heart." Then he said: "Fink I will join you". So he did." What we need now" he said "is a bit of good old music". With that he proceeded to play proper old sing along tunes on his record player. By now, we had finished our drinks and handed back our glasses which were immediately replenished. In no time at all, with his window now wide open, the three of us were serenading all and sundry from ten floors up. However, this came to a sudden end when our foreman's' head appeared unexpectedly, looking down at us from the flat roof above. "Enjoying yourselves lads"? He enquired. "Sorry guv", I said. "We were cold and he gave us a drop of scotch and I'm afraid we got carried away a bit". "A bit! He exclaimed. "A bit! You've got half of Canning Town complaining, and it would not be so bad if you could bleeding well sing. Now get yourselves off that scaffold and get back to the yard and sober up". Of course, we should have got the sack, but after a really good rollicking he let us off with a very stern warning.

Twenty-Seven:
Council Officer

I was on my tools for about three years and I could never quite figure out whether I was a good tradesman or not because I was promoted very quickly. It happened one Christmas, in a pub where we had all gathered for our annual do. I was approached by one of the managers, who said: "Johnny I have heard some good things about you and how well you get on with the tenants". "That's nice to hear" I replied. He went on to say that he was leading to a particular point, as follows: "There is a vacant post for a Property Inspector and I think you are the man for it. What do you think of the idea?" I did not need any second thoughts, for I had often seen these fellas walking around with their clip boards, all suited and booted, and I thought to myself at the time, now that's a job I would like. "Yes please" I answered. He was glad that I was keen, but went on to say that good I would still have to have an interview to see if I could come up to scratch. "Not a problem" I replied. "Tell me where and when and I will be there: and thank you." Here we go again, I thought: the start of something new once more. I'm pleased to say that the interview went well and I was offered the job.

I was based in an office in East Ham. My job was to arrange work for all trades employed by the council. My area had six thousand properties and covered an area from East Ham right the way down to North Woolwich. My Manager was a young fella called Tony, who was as bright as a button. I knew right away that he would go to the top in Local government and I was proved correct. We hit it off straight away, and at the beginning of my first day, he invited me into his office for a cuppa and a chat. Like me he was young and still had a lot to learn, especially about the East End, so we agreed he would learn from me and I would learn from him regarding my new role as a council officer. He set high standards insisting that I would always act in a way that did not let him or the council down. This I agreed to and said I would do my best. My first assignment was in the prefab estate in Beckton. I was very smartly turned out in a navy blue blazer and light grey flannel trousers. I knocked on the front entrance door of one of these prefabs, and a woman opened and asked who I was? I was just about to answer when a massive hairy Alsatian dog, covered in coal dust, came bounding out of the coal shed making a bee line for my backside. The tenant then said "It's alright mate he is just being friendly". By this time, he had both front paws on my clean white shirt and my immaculate grey trousers were now smothered in coal dust. Obviously, I could make any more calls in this condition, so I returned to the office. On seeing the state I was in Tony asked me what happened and I explained in some detail. Then he expressed the hope that I had remembered what he said about being a representative of the council and conducted myself accordingly. I replied: "Oh rest assured I did Tony, but I suddenly found I could speak fluent French". "Really" he said. "Now go home and get changed".

During my time in that job, I must have visited hundreds of homes. Some were spotless and would ask you to remove your shoes at the door. Others were the opposite and protective clothing would be the order of the day. When encountering this kind of home I would always inform the tenant that unless it was cleaned up I would not be sending anyone to carry out repairs. However I went to one very old lady who was seeking some new taps for her bath. I went into her bathroom to have a look to see what I could do, and said to her "Sorry love I cannot do it". She replied: "I thought you would say that." This was probably because, at that time, property inspectors were notorious for keeping a tight rein on council expenditures. The reason I said no was that the bath had hardly any white enamel left on it through being constantly cleaned, whilst the taps on the hand basin and bath were brass and were highly polished. Everything in that bathroom was spotlessly clean but very well worn. So I said: "No love you cannot have new taps, but what you can have is a brand new, totally decorated, fully equipped bathroom". "Thank you young man," she replied, with a little tear welling up in her eyes. I think I was the talk of the town amongst the other property inspectors, of whom one was heard to say, "If he carries on like that he will bankrupt the council!"

One working day, I called on one of my tenants whom I shall call Ginger, about a repair that needed attention. I had known this lady for a long while. We sat down and she started by saying, that she supposed I had heard about the 'old man', her husband. I said: "No mate. What's happened?"

She replied: "He has been banged up again, this time for a long un". "How long?" I said. "Ten years", was her reply. "What did he get done for this time? I asked. "A naughty one", she answered. "armed robbery". We had quite a long talk, but was aware that I felt there was little I could say to make things better, so in the end, I made my excuses and said I had to go. However, before leaving, I suggested she do me and herself a favour by taking down the sawn off shotgun hanging up over the fireplace, because if she were to get a visit from the 'old bill' she might find herself joining her old man. It seems she had no idea that she was committing two offences: firstly, it was illegal to have a fire arm unless licensed, and secondly, there was only one reason to saw off the barrel of a shotgun, and her husband was living proof of it. Years later, I asked her what had become of it and she said she had thrown it into the Thames when crossing over on the Woolwich Ferry.

Over the years I carried out many of my inspections on the very large prefab estate in Beckton. These homes were first built as a short term remedial measure, prior to more robust houses coming along later. They were nearly thirty years old when I took them over and were beginning to show real signs of wear. On calling at an address one day, I heard the lady of the house call out to her husband: "Oh here he comes Mr Promise". This may have been because it was difficult to carry out a proper repair on the prefabs in view of their age and nature of their construction, and I had needed to explain this to tenants, probably including this lady. However, it really got to me, so I went back to the office, had a meeting with Tony, my manager, and told him that because of the condition of those prefabs I and the council were losing credibility. "So what do you suggest he asked?" I expressed the opinion that when they cannot be properly repaired, we should begin to get a programme in place to get them demolished. He asked if they were really that bad, and I said that in a lot of cases they were.

At that time we had a very good Chair of Housing, Bill Watts to whom Tony wrote explaining the whole situation. The Chair then called for meeting and asked that both Tony and I attend. The outcome was that I was to submit a report, which outlined the defects of every prefab I judged to be no longer reparable to the standard required by the council. Such buildings would then be taken down. I carried out the task with gusto, and in the end the estate looked like a patch work quilt. At this stage, it was not too hard for the chair to put to the committee that the whole estate be demolished and the tenants rehoused, and it all came about because the tenant called me Mr Promise.

At that time I was also a council tenant and my philosophy started from the expectation that the Council would keep my home in good order, and because I was now part of that service, I would do my best to ensure the tenants were treated according to the same standards.

One of my colleagues in the office, Sid, was a retired, formerly high ranking policeman. He was a very distinguished looking man, well over six foot in height, slightly portly and with wavy silver hair. He was the rent arrears officer, and amongst his gifts was that of a great story teller. He would have us all in stiches at the staff Christmas meal with stories of police days. We got on like a house on fire and would often go for lunch to a pub called the Sherlock Holmes, which was very near Trafalgar Square. On very rare occasions we would go to the Savoy for a gin and tonic or two, and taking into account the nice bottle of wine we had in the pub we were feeling a little jolly. Sid suggested we go to the Ritz for afternoon tea, which I judged to be a good idea. Sid, who like me appreciated nice clothes, looked down at my feet and remarked that I had on a very fine pair of shoes. I said: "Glad you like them Sid, bought them in New Bond Street, and they cost a lot of money". The shoes in question were brown leather brogues and they were the most comfortable shoes I have ever had. But I think I must have been gilding the lily a little bit about the shoes, because I saw Sid was beginning to wilt.

On arriving at the Ritz, Sid looking his most regal, walked up to the Head Waiter and said "Table for two, please". The man enquired "Have you booked sir? "Sorry I haven't" Sid replied. The Head waiter then replied in a very haughty tone: "Sir, this is the Ritz, surely you do not expect to get a table without booking". Sid replied: "That maybe the case my man, but have you seen his shoes?" With that, Sid took me by the elbow and led me out, leaving a very puzzled looking Head Waiter.

Twenty-Eight:
Almighty slap

The year was nineteen seventy six. I had been a Christian for nine years, went to church regularly, read my bible daily, said my prayers every night and tried to be true to the faith in my behaviour. All in all supposedly toeing the line, but unlike others who became Christians around the same time as me, I did not feel that I was being used in carrying out anything that indicated I was indeed a Christian. Others were leading groups, or actually preaching from the front, but for me nothing.

One day one of my mates came to work in a very smart suit. I remarked: "That a nice bit of clobber where did you get it?" "From a mate of mine" he replied." I asked whether worked in a shop, or was perhaps a tailor. He answered: "Neither. He is a delivery man who has got a deal going with somebody in the warehouse". I said: "So they are hooky?" He replied: "Yeah, still interested?" My response was to tell him "Yeah, why not. Fetch some in tomorrow and let me have a look". (My walk around St Pauls Cathedral had started). The next day he duly arrived with a parcel. They were really nice suits and the price was very reasonable, so I bought three. Then my contact said: "Johnny I am packing it in. I have got a new job, so I won't be able to keep contact with the fella in the warehouse. Do you want to take my place?" "Not half", I replied.

Before I continue, I need to stress that I had no valid reason for making this decision. I had a good, well paid job with excellent prospects, but for no other reason than greed, I still decided to give it a crack. In no time at all I got my hands on dozens of suits, which sold in no time at all, because of their high quality and cheap price. Whether or not the guys who bought the suits from me guessed they were stolen, I don't know. They didn't ask and I didn't tell them. One thing I do know is that we had the smartest council officers in London.

Now I believe in God and I also believe in the devil, and he had hooked me good and proper: quite a prize a so called Christian. He seemed to make it very easy for me to become 'good at being bad'. In a matter of weeks, the word went round amongst other people who were involved in a similar game, that I was 'at it'. So, I quickly progressed into the world of dealing with stolen property, fencing. I never dealt with anything major. It was just small stuff that was easy to get rid of. This went on for a few months and I was earning a nice little living on the side.

Roy Trevivian was my vicar at the time. One night he came round to my home and said: "Johnny we need to talk". I asked what about. He replied: "I think you know". "Go on then", I said. He went on to say, "Well, a little birdie has told me that you are up to a bit of mischief." I replied: "Yes, you are right. But it's nothing major; just a little bit of bent stuff on the side". I had never seen Roy angry before, but this time he exploded. "A little bit on the side! Have you any idea how many people you have let down? Can you not see them now, saying is that how a supposed Christian behaves? What about all those who helped you along the way? Skipper, Bobby, Roger and the whole congregation of the Mayflower: but most important, you have made your Saviour the Lord Jesus sad, because he did save you from sin but you have gone over to the other side again." Just before he left, his parting words were: "Johnny you are walking a very dangerous path. Do not try and con God because he will not allow it. Do you understand?" That was on a Tuesday. On the Saturday, two policemen arrived with a search warrant. They didn't have to look far. I had just had a delivery, so my home looked like Marks and Spencer. It appears that one of my neighbours had grassed me up having contacted the police about my shenanigans. One of the officers asked a number of questions, the main thrust being to find out the names of my suppliers? I replied: "You have had one easy touch, but I am afraid that's where it ends. You will get no names out of me".

So that was it. I was taken to the Abbey Arms police station and charged with handling stolen goods and I was granted bail. If anything, I am a realist. I had been playing with fire and there is a distinct probability that I was going to get severely burnt, which turned out to be the case. The first thing I did was to inform Tony, my manager of my predicament. He replied "I thought you were up to something, but I just thought it was a bit of East End ducking and diving." I said: "No Tony. I am sorry, mate. It is a bit more serious than that. I gave him the whole picture and replied that we should play it by ear and see what happens, and this was exactly what we did.

A few weeks later I appeared at East Ham Magistrates' Court, but it was decided that it was too big a case for that court, so my next port of call was Snaresbrook Crown court. I appeared there at ten am on the twenty third of December nineteen seventy six. Accompanying me was my Warden Vicar, the Rev Roger Sainsbury.

Before going to the Court, I rang Tony and Sid telling them both that I would see them in the Hammers' Club for our rearranged Christmas lunch, because I was so convinced that, being my first senior offence, I would receive a hefty fine and a suspended sentence. So, into the box I went. The crime sheet – which was pretty serious- was read out, and I was asked whether I pleaded guilty or not guilty". I replied: "Guilty", and Roger Sainsbury was then invited to get up and say his piece on my behalf.

The time came for the Judge to pass sentence. His opening words were: "John Ringwood I believe you are an intelligent man, and you knew exactly what you were doing. So I am going to make an example of you. I sentence you to twelve months' imprisonment. Take him down." I had been waiting for the word suspended but it didn't happen. Therefore, down to the holding cells I went. Later in the day they allowed Brenda to visit me. "Sorry mate" I said. She replied: "That's OK darling. But I will tell you this now. You will not be in there for long". I said "Brenda don't build your hopes up mate that was a High Court judge who gave me the sentence". With that the Warden asked her to leave. I think another reason for such a sentence was the fact that I did not help the police with their enquiries.

At about seven pm, I was handcuffed to a young skinhead. We were then taken outside to a coach, which we boarded. Almost as soon as we sat in our seats this young idiot started to tell me how hard and smart he was. I let him go on for a while, and then said: "Listen mate, I don't know what planet you are on but we are both on our way to prison, so we are not smart, are we? As to how tough you are, I could not care less. So please shut the f**k up". I think he got the message because there wasn't a peep out of him for the rest of the journey. I asked the guard who was accompanying us where we were going. He said it would be Wormwood Scrubs, but before we got there we called at a number of other courts to pick up some more men who had been convicted that day.

When we arrived at the prison, we were taken to a reception area, where we were told to strip naked. This was for the doctor to give us the once over. After a very few basic questions about our health, we were told to put our clothes into a cardboard box. We were then issued with prison clothing. From reception, I was taken to "A" wing which was the wing for new arrivals. Finally I was taken into a cell and told to make up my bed. Already in the cell were two other men who had also received sentences that day. To say the amenities were minimal is to put it mildly. There were two bunks on one side and one single on the other with a small wall mounted notice board. Underneath was a bucket which was used as a toilet. The unwritten rule was this was only to be used for urine, because it was only emptied in the morning, which was commonly known as "slops out". On occasions, for whatever reason the bucket was used for the other purpose, which meant until morning the cell was left with the side effects.

By now I was beginning to hit rock bottom, suddenly realising that all I had worked for had now gone down the river. But, before I continue with my 'woe is me' theme, I am reminded of what an old lag once told me, which was: "If you can't do the time, don't do the crime". So with that mind set, I thought to myself, OK Johnny boy, you created all this, now take it on the chin and get on with it. Finally the lights were put out, but there was no sleep for me.'A' wing was a very noisy place, and even after lights out men were calling to each other. It was after twelve when I heard the man on the top bunk scratching, which continued all night, along with the noisy masturbation of the man on the lower bunk.

The next morning after breakfast and Slops out, I was told that the doctor wanted to see me in the medical room, so a warden accompanied me there, then I was left alone waiting in a side room. Whilst I was in there I got talking to a fella who was the spitting image of Rocky Balboa's trainer from the Rocky films. I asked him what he was in for and he replied: "Gun running". I asked how long a sentence he got and he replied: "A long 'un, but it's not too bad, I've got two of my sons in here with me!". Finally, with my imagination running riot, I got to see the doctor. After inviting me to sit down, he said: "Now, I am sorry about this, but one of the men in your cell has got scabies, which is quite contagious, so he has been put into an isolation ward and your cell will have to be decontaminated". I said: "Just a minute, surely this should have been detected when like all of us, he was naked." He answered: "That's where the problem arises. I misdiagnosed it as psoriasis. It was only when I read his medical report that I realised my mistake." "So where does that leave me?" I asked. He replied:

"I assume there was no bodily contact? "You can bloody well rest assured on that doctor" I replied. "Then there should not be a problem" he said. "However should your skin show any signs of a problem then you must report it immediately?"

I was then taken back to my cell, to which I and the others were confined for twenty three and a half hours a day. During the day the man on the lower bunk, who was large and ginger, struck up a conversation, by asking me what I had been 'done' for? I explained that it was dealing with stolen goods. I asked him the same question, and he answered: "I should not be here. I was falsely accused of interfering with my seven year old niece". I said that I supposed he had pleaded not guilty? "Of course" he replied. "But a jury found you guilty" I said. "Yes, but they were a bunch of idiots", he answered. By now I was beginning to boil. All I wanted to do was to smash this lowlife to pieces, but I had to bide my time. On the way down to dinner, I approached one of the guards and told him the story and said "If you don't get him out of my cell, I am going to blot my copy book big time". Within half an hour the man was put into the segregation unit, where he should have been assigned in the first place, along with all the other prisoners who had committed similar offences.

So all in all, I was not a happy cookie. I was not on my own for long. The first fella that came in was from Wales. It appears he was down in London as a corner man in a boxing match that was held at York Hall, a famous boxing venue. In his own words he explained that whilst he was down here, he would look around and see if there were any golden opportunities around. The one that got him into trouble was a large window of a jewellers shop. On display were trays of very expensive watches. So the night before the match he carried out a smash and grab, but unluckily for him a patrol car was just passing as he did it. The two patrol officers tried to arrest him but he floored them. But by now, reinforcements turned up and he was finally subdued and arrested. He was charged with robbery, and assault and battery, and because of his previous record he got five years. The other man allocated to the cell was a small time crook who was always in and out of jail.

I could put up with basic food and confinement but what was really getting to me was that I could not shower or maintain a decent standard of basic hygiene. I went in on Friday and the following Sunday was Christmas day. The church inside the prison was very large and could accommodate a fair sized congregation. Anyone who wanted to attend the Christmas service was allowed to do so and I put my name down. People from our wing who wanted to go were assembled in the exercise yard. From there, we were marched into the church. Just as I was to take my place the man from the medical room Rocky's trainer, who was also the chapel candle man beckoned me over and whispered: "Get right in the middle. They are filming for the television programme, Panorama in here". So, right in the middle I positioned myself, hoping to avoid the cameras, but it did not make any difference, because a few months after I was released it was shown on television, and to my horror the camera homed right in on me. I suspect it was because my expression was extremely forlorn, so any chance of keeping my stay at the Scrubbs at a low profile had vanished. It was altogether a brilliant service, but the thing that impressed me most, was that the music for the service was provided by the Salvation Army. They had sacrificed their Christmas day, for what some would call us lowlifes. It is something I have never forgotten.

One of the visits I had was from my Mum and Dad, I was always the apple of my Dad's eye, and as I got promoted at work, I could see how proud he was. This was particularly clear on one day, when I called in at his local pub, outside of which he also had a Jellied Eel stall. I recollect that he was sitting at a table in the bar surrounded by his mates. I walked in all suited and booted, and I saw the look of pride in his eyes when he introduced me. But sitting now, on the other side of the table, in the visiting room of this infamous prison, those eyes that were once filled with pride were now filled with tears, and I was so sorry.

In terms of prison process, the next thing that happened was that each person was categorised to decide where they would be sent to serve the rest of their sentence. The more serious cases were often kept in the Scrubs, whilst others, including me, were sent to various suitable locations. My destination was an open prison.

On the morning of our departure for the open prison, which was in East Church on the Isle of Sheppey, we were given our on clothes to wear for the journey, which was once again in an ordinary coach. On arriving at the prison we were taken to the reception area, and told to undress. As I was queuing, I noticed the warden talking to the inmate behind the counter and he was looking and pointing in my direction. When I got to the counter I handed in my clothing and was issued with the prison uniform. Just as I was about to leave the inmate said: "There is a job going in here, and with a little wink he emphasized, and you want it DON'T you?" I thought to myself that I had got nothing to lose, so I replied: "Yes of course, thank you".

Then we were taken to our sleeping quarters. They were huts which closely resembled the ones I had been in during my time in the army at Purfleet. The ablution facilities were by far a vast improvement on the closed prison I had just left. I think there were about twenty of us in the hut, all of whom seemed to be okay. When they found out that I had got a job in reception, they wanted to know who I had slipped a few quid to. I said: "Why? Is it that good a job? They replied: "You are kidding! It's the best job in the nick!"

One by one, all members of the new intake had to report to the Governor of the prison. On arriving at his office, I knocked on his door and a voice called out to come in, which I did. He beckoned me to sit down on a chair in front of his desk. He introduced himself, and then said "Ringwood this I an open prison, which means there are no perimeter walls to stop you absconding, so you are in a position of trust. If you betray that trust and try to escape, you will be dealt with very severely. Do you get my drift?" I replied: "Sir, I am an ex-merchant seaman and soldier and as such I am used to obeying orders. Therefore, you have my word that I will comply with the rules and regulations of this place". He replied: "Good. Glad to hear it. You can go now".

The next morning I reported to the reception building, and the two cons that were already working there said: "Hello mate, welcome. Your first job is to make the tea." "No problem", I replied. Then I was introduced to the two wardens who run the place. The first thing that impressed me was when the older one of the two said: "We are on first names terms here. My name is Bill and my colleague here is Bert, so what do we call you?" "Johnny", I replied. "Okay, Johnny boy we are a tight team so let's keep it that way. Alright? "I will do my best Bill", I replied. There were quite a few office duties, but nothing that involved anything of a confidential nature. As a sign of trust Bill said: "Johnny, the warden's canteen is along the front of the camp and every morning, I want you go and get anything that me and Bert want, such as sandwiches and cigarettes, and take your time, there is no rush". As well as being a nice guy, Bill was giving me a chance to be on my own for a little while, something I had been longing for.

On the way to the canteen, there was a grass verge that was out of sight of the camp, and it was on this verge that I broke down for the first time, fully realising what a horrible mess I had made of everything. So,I did the only thing I could do and that was to get down on my knees and pray, and it was a prayer of deep sorrow. "Lord, I have been given many chances, both earthly and spiritually, and yet I decided to throw them all away just for a quick few quid". Then I made a promise that if, and it was a big 'if' "Lord, you could find it in your heart to forgive me and give me a second chance, then I would dedicate the rest of my life to carrying out your will." Now, anyone reading this will think to him or herself, that I got what I deserved, and I could not agree more, but I have to tell you that that prayer was answered, as you will find out later.

One of my designated jobs was to get the cardboard boxes which contained the convicts' clothing, down from the shelves. The contents of these boxes would be needed by those who were leaving or who were attending the Appeal Court on that day. In the storeroom I found an old ironing board and an electric iron. In the main, the boxed contents were in a very crumpled condition, and I took the clothes to be used that day and set about pressing and ironing them. Bill noticed what I was doing and said: "John, you don't have to do that." I replied If it isn't a problem, I would like to do it". He answered: "No. It's up to you". But why are you doing it?" I said: " Well, I just want to give them half a chance. I just don't want anyone turning up at the Appeal Court not looking a bit decent". Then I said: "Bill. Just out of curiosity, as I was lining up on my first day here I noticed you talking to one of the cons here, and at the same time looking and pointing at me. What was all that about?" He answered: "To tell you the truth, I was impressed by how smart and clean you were, and my thinking was that if you take that much care about your appearance, then you would be an asset to us in reception, and I have got to tell you that, so far I am not disappointed". "Thanks Bill that's nice to hear", I replied.

During my time in the open prison I received a number of visits, most of which were from my family. But I was really pleased when my manager Tony and my good friend Sid turned up one afternoon. First thing Sid said was: "That was very inconsiderate of you not turning up for our lunch at the Hammers club". I replied: "Sorry Sid. I had a request from her Majesty to dine elsewhere". The conversation drifted into what I might have in mind for the future once I was released, and I answered: "To tell you the truth, I haven't got a clue". I did not know at that time that they knew about my pending appeal. Later I learned that they had contacted Brenda, who informed them what she had been up to.

Sometimes in life if you are very fortunate. You will meet people who are very special: Tony and Sid were two such people. I say this because once they had heard from Brenda, they began to make inroads with regards to reinstating me back into my old job. But of course I knew nothing of this.

Twenty-Nine:
The Appeal

The reader may remember that when my wife Brenda spoke to me in the holding cells at Snaresbrook Court, she said: "You won't be in here long John". To that end, and unbeknown to me, she started enquiring as to how you went about setting up an appeal. Fortunately, the chairperson of the Mayflower at that time was a High Court Judge, so it was a good place to start.

A little while before I was arrested, my eldest son, Terry, had a very serious fall of some twenty feet. So bad were his injuries that the head nurse in the London Hospital said after his first assessment that Brenda and I should prepare for the worst. Thanks be to God, he pulled through but was left with some life long side effects. Brenda went to see the lead Surgeon and explained my predicament and emphasised that, at this time Terry would really benefit if I were around to support him. She must have been very convincing because he agreed to come on board, and wrote a letter of support accordingly. Her next port of call was the West Ham boxing club and she had the same effect on an ex Army Captain who was the Chair of the club. Then the Skipper, David Shepherd, who was now a Bishop got to hear, and also became a supporter, along with the Rev. Roy Trevivian..

Collectively, an Appeal against the harshness of my sentence was put together and a date was set for it to be heard at the Appeal Courts in London. A week or so before the hearing I was sent for by the Warden who's responsibility it was to brief me on the proceedings. His first question to me was: "Who are you?" I replied: "John Ringwood". He said: "I know that, but I am asking you who are you really?" I replied: "I don't understand. What do you mean? He said: "You must be a 'somebody', because the only person missing amongst your supporters is the Queen". I was as mystified as he was because I too didn't know how many people Brenda had got to support me. Come the day of the appeal, I was told that I would be taken into solitary during the day and from there I would either return to the hut or be released. I wasn't at all sure how it would go, so I just in case I had a good result, I said goodbye to the boys in the hut and a fond farewell to those in reception. I went into the solitary cell at about ten am and it was not until seven thirty pm that the warden said: "Put on your own clothes, you are going home". I was escorted to the main gate, on the outside of which was my brilliant wife Brenda, and my good Christian Brother Bobby, who drove me home.

Brenda told me later that she was accompanied at the appeal court by, Tony, Sid and Roy, thereby giving me another lesson in loyalty. I have a photo in my possession taken of Brenda sitting on a chair in our living room, when I was first imprisoned. I have never seen her more broken, and every time I look at that photo I am reminded how much hurt I brought onto her and my sons. I vowed then that never again would I bring about such suffering.

The woman who informed the police of my illegal activities was looked down on and condemned by many of our neighbours, because rightly or wrongly, it is an unwritten law in the East End, that you do not do that sort of thing. But I thank God for that woman, because if she had not done it, I was heading for the big time in the criminal world. You see, I was very gifted at pushing stolen goods. In addition, I would pay on the button, to anyone who wanted me to dispose of their stolen goods, so the rogues were lining up to trade.

Thirty: Fiftieth Birthday

Since my stay in Her Majesties prisons I vowed that I would in the future always stay within the boundaries of the Law. However it is said if you want to make God smile. 'Make a plan'

This particular incident took place in a Chinese Restaurant called The Young Friends in the West India Dock, Road Limehouse. It was here that I, my family and a few friends were having a meal to celebrate my fiftieth birthday. At that time both my Mum and Brenda's Dad were still alive. It was a lovely occasion until it was marred by two couples on a nearby table, who I guess were in their mid-thirties. I noticed that they getting stuck into amount of wine and as they were doing so their voices increased in volume.

The problem occurred when the conversations stopped and was replaced by the two men who started singing dirty and lewd rugby songs that should have been confined to locker rooms.

I looked at my Mum and Brenda's Dad both of whom were looking very embarrassed, I also noticed the angry looks on my three sons faces. Steve my middle son is a pretty tough East Ender and who like me has a short fuse. He looked at me and gave a little nod in the direction of the songsters, I gave a little wave back indicating to leave it, he did for a while but they continued, so he stood up went over to their table and asked them to knock it off, one of them stood up to Steve to "f**k off" and gave him a shove. Steve responded by giving him a short jab to the stomach and a left hook to the jaw, the other man tried to hit Steve but by this time I was on my feet and I got stuck into him. What followed was like a wild west film with tables going over in all directions, until finally the two couples beat a hasty retreat.

The manager who was a friend had witnessed all of this, and graciously agreed to let us continue with our celebrations. So alongside with the other people in the restaurant together we put all the tables and chairs back in their original positions, the only sign that there had been a fracas was a splash of Soya sauce up one of the walls.

After leaving the restaurant and unbeknown to us, the two couples went along to the nearby Limehouse Police Station. Where they informed the officer on the enquiries counter, "that they had been assaulted by a crowd of people in the Young Friends Chinese restaurant".

By then we had begun to continue with our meal, when suddenly two Police Officers entered. They spoke to the manager and asked "if there had been any trouble there that evening", he replied "nothing really except a bit of a row".

One of the officers replied. "We believe it was a bit more serious than that, and we have some people back at the station who claim they have been assaulted in here tonight". He then looked around at the people seated and pointed to Steve and said "you fit the description of the one of the people involved, so you are under arrest". I stood up and said I want also to come along to the station to ensure fair play is that okay, this they agreed to.

So along to Limehouse nick we went, on arriving they told Steve to empty his pockets, the Sergeant then turned to me now empty your also, hang on a minute mate I said I am here as a witness, no I am sorry you fit the other description of a man involved.

We were then banged up in a cell, I turned to Steve and said here I am trying to walk along the straight and narrow and what happens, to celebrate my birthday I am back in the nick.

We were in the cell for a couple of hours when the Sergeant came in and said the two men want to press charges for assault, but before I proceed I want to hear your side of the story. So I told him in full exactly what happened, his reply was "the barstards" But before I make any final decisions I am going to speak to the owner of the restaurant. Which he did, and I am glad to say he explained to the officer exactly as I had done. But he also said that if these people still wanted to proceed with their allegations, then he in turn would want them charged with disturbing the peace and causing damage to his property. About four-am the officer returned to the cell and informed me and Steve that after a conversation with two couples they had decided to back off. He also told them that in the light of the conversations that he had had with me and the restaurant owner that they were lucky is was not them that should have been locked up. I said that's good then so I suppose we can be released then, he replied "I am sorry fellas but I cannot do that until all my paperwork is complete"

It was around eight am when I got home it was then I finally got to blow out my Fifty Birthday candles

Thirty-One:
Back to the Mayflower

On the first Sunday following my release I went to church. This was both to give thanks to God and to say how sorry I was. But I had forgotten these were Canning Town people who had hearts as big as shovels. So it was hugs and kisses and welcome back from everyone in the congregation. Amongst those gathered was Pip Wilson the Leader in the Mayflower's Youth Club. As we were having a cup of tea after the service, he asked me if I had ever thought of becoming a Youth Worker? "No, not really" I replied. "Well, give it some thought" he said. "But in the meantime I wonder if you would speak to the Canning Town kids who use the Club?" I asked what about and he said that he would leave that one up to me, but that he thought I would know where he was coming from. I did, and so I agreed. On the following Wednesday evening at about nine a-clock, on his God's Spot, Pip got all the young men and women assembled in the large hall of the club. Then he introduced me, although quite a few already knew me through my three sons. They had no idea what I was going to talk about, except that Pip had introduced me as a Christian brother.

I thanked him and said to those gathered: "Good evening. Pip Called me a Christian and I am, but not a very good one". I went on to give them the full story of what had happened over the last year or so. I was pushing on an open door because quite a few of the young fellas amongst those seated, had themselves had run-ins with the police. "So I said. "Why am I telling you all this? Well some of you already have had advice from your probation officers on the error of your ways and the likely consequences. Well, I am not a probation officer. I am out of the same stable as you, and I can guarantee that I would leave you at the starting block with regards to being streetwise and how to duck and dive. But as cute and clever as I thought I was, I was not smart enough to beat the Law: and I will tell you this; I will never try to again. So where does that leave me and some of you? As far as I am concerned, I have been given a second chance and I am going to grab that chance with both hands: and where does that leave you? My advice to some of you, for whom this talk may ring a few bells, is to take a page out of my book and couple that sharp East End brain with some further education, which is readily available if you want it. In other words, just give yourselves a long term chance". The following day Pip thanked me, but I said "I pray my words were not falling on deaf ears". "Me too", Pip replied.

In nineteen eighty, a new Mayflower Youth Club was erected and in one part of it was a small, weight training area. I had been pumping iron for many years, so I approached Pip with an idea. If I were to get a training qualification related to this, did he think that it would meet the criteria for working with young people. He replied that he thought that it would be a great idea, which would certainly appeal to the macho minded youngsters. Thus, yet another area of development was on the horizon. Not only did I get qualified, but the local authority also hired me as part of the rehabilitation service for wayward youngsters. I hasten to say this was carried out during the evenings, and I still keep in touch with some of the boys and girls who had belonged to the weight training venture.

The official opening of the new Youth Club was carried out on the day by Her Majesty the Queen Mother. I was told to be on stand-by in case her Majesty came to my area, which eventually happened, I had been told to have the youngsters carrying out their normal activity. In one area, one fifteen year old girl was bench pressing a weight, and her majesty asked her what the exercise was for. The young girl replied "I'm trying to increase me bust size miss". Her Majesty graciously replied, with a raised eyebrow "Oh how lovely". On, going upstairs her Majesty went into the games room where some boys were playing snooker. On her arrival, one of the cheeky cockneys asked her if she wanted a game. Without hesitation, she picked up a billiard cue and potted a black, to the cheers of everyone around. We learnt later that her Majesty had acquired these skills in one of her homes that had been converted to accommodate wounded airman, with whom she often played snooker or billiards. A photograph of her skill, as displayed at the Mayflower was prominently featured in a number of newspapers.

Thirty-Two:
A new start

I had been home for about a week when I received a phone call from Tony, telling me that he had arranged for a meeting with the Chairman of Housing. So I went along, not building up my hopes too much, but praying a lot. There were only three of us present; the Chair, Tony and myself. I had thought this might have been a committee decision, but this was not the case. Bill, the Chair who, incidentally was a real East Ender came good. He said: "Johnny you have been a complete prat. Do you agree?" "Totally", I replied. He said: "I have got to tell you that if it was not for Tony and Sid speaking so well of you, you would not have stood a chance of getting your job back". He went on to say that after a lot of consideration, and providing that I kept my nose clean, I could start back to work the following Monday. I thanked him and told him that I would never let him down, and I kept to that promise. On Monday, after leaving the office, I went down to the works depot to pick up where I had left off. I was greeted extremely warmly by the men and woman who worked there, many of them saying how good it was to see me back. I thanked them and said that I had better get out there and get them some work. So, armed with a sheath of papers regarding tenants whose homes needed repairs done, off I trotted.

As well as getting praise from the tenants when they got what they wanted, there were times when I took a lot of stick, because I had to refuse them. But on the whole, I really liked that job, because basically I am a people person and as such I was privileged to meet and visit the homes of many hundreds of them. I am pleased to say that I soon settled back into the old routine.

About a year later Tony was offered a post of Director of Housing in another London Borough, and Sid was due to retire. This was good for them but very sad for me because I was going to lose two of the nicest and most loyal friends any man could ever have. On the day of their departure, a farewell office party was arranged and off they went, with really good wishes for the future.

Thirty-Three:
Health and Safety

At around this time, significant new legislation was put into place. It was entitled The Health and Safety at Work Act 1974, and Newham council decided, at committee level to create a new section to implement it. One day, I received a letter from the then Head of Management Services, whose office was in the East Ham Town Hall, asking if I would be interested in becoming a part of this new team. As it was a promotion, I replied that I certainly would be interested. So, an interview was arranged, with Pip Mortlock, the head of Management Services. He was 'old school' and got straight to the point by saying: "This Act is a new one to all of us, so there will be a big learning curve for everyone concerned". In order to conform to the Act it will mean that Newham Council requires all of the officers involved to gain professional qualifications in this field. To do so will take a lot of studying both in council time and in your own. Are you still up for it for it son?" "If offered the job I will do my best" I answered. "Good", he replied. "I will give you two weeks so that you can tie up any loose ends from your present job". Then he gave me a starting date, and another round of farewell parties took place both in my office and the works depot.

On the given date I set off for the Town Hall, and on arriving I was introduced to my new boss Ron, and two other appointed Safety Officers, Helen and Mike, both of whom were University Graduates. I was still not quite sure how I was going to fit in with all this brain power.

Mike had a brilliant, scientific back ground and Helen was an excellent scribe, and as we progressed I began to see a pattern forming, especially between Mike and I who were carrying out inspections. He would get the overall angle and I would grasp the nitty gritty common sense side of it. Helen's role was to produce the reams of the paper work required by the Act, such as Safety Policies, Corporate strategies, Risk Assessments, to mention just a few. All three of us had to attend a College in Barking one day a week. It goes without saying that both Mike and Helen found the studying side far easier than I did, especially the maths side of it. I had a problem with fractions and decimals and was completely lost when the lecturer started talking about moments and algebra. But in the end all three of us became Members of a Health and Safety Institution, which enabled me, for the first time in our Ringwood's history, to put letters after my name. (Good old Mrs Abercrombie!)

Our inspections covered every area in which our workforce was employed. They ranged from building sites to old folk's homes and from Schools to the Mortuary. I remember the first time I ever went to the Mortuary. It was one visit I hadn't been looking forward to. The first thing I was confronted with when the entering the autopsy area was an elderly lady, fully prepared for the man who carried out the autopsies. On seeing my worried look, the young fella in charge of the morgue said: "John, this is what this place is all about. Come closer and take a good look, because this dear lady is in a far better condition than some of the corpses we have to deal with on other occasions". So I did just that, and the strangest thought came into my head. It occurred to me that just a few weeks earlier, this lady would have been pulling her skirt over her knees for modesty's sake, and here she lay as naked as the day that she was born. I felt utter respect for her, and expressed my thanks to the mortician for his encouragement.

A few years later, I visited the same Morgue, which by now had fallen way below the standards required. This meant that I had no alternative other than to serve a prohibition notice, which meant it would either have to be improved to meet current standards or be shut down.

Over the years I had served a number of these notices and my boss Ron had developed a twitch, similar that of Inspector Cluso in the Peter Sellers Pink Panther film. Every time I informed him that I had served another notice, this twitch would become more pronounced. When I told him about the Morgue, I thought his head was going to come off. "What about the deceased?" he asked." I said: Well, because it's not too hot a day, we took them out of the fridges and laid them down on the lawn at the back." "You did what?" He screamed. "Nah. Only kidding Ron". I replied. "Everything is still in situ until we can make alternative arrangements." He replied: "You are one sick man. Now, get out of my office".

On another occasion, Pip our Head of Service, went on long term sick leave and was greatly missed. After a few months, the word went round that he was returning on the following Monday. Hoping he would return with the same sense of humour, I decided to welcome him back in a particular way. I went over to East Ham College and borrowed a full size skeleton, which I clothed, adding a yellow safety helmet as the finishing touch. I placed the skeleton behind Pip's desk, sitting in his chair. I rested an arm on the desk and put a pen in the hand. Then I propped up a big notice which read: 'Really good to see you back Pip, but do you not think it was a tad too early?' I think the whole of the Town Hall staff viewed my caper.

Just before Pip's return, I retired to my adjacent office. I heard him opening his door and there was a pregnant pause: then he roared out "RINGWOOD get your arse in here". I have still no idea how he knew it was me. I went in and asked in all innocence: "What's a matter Pip?" With his finger pointing at my art work, he said: "That's the matter you little git!" However, all the time he had a great big smile on his face. I gave him a wink a said: "Good to have you back, Pip".

One of my health and safety inspections was at a school whose Head Teacher was a nun called Sister Mary, and I was accompanied by a young trainee. On arriving at the school we were taken immediately to Sister Mary's office. Looking at me with a very grim expression on her face, she said "Sit down. We need to talk." We both did as instructed. She said: "Right. I want you to understand from the start that I do not want my school to be disrupted in any way, by your so-called inspection: and I have heard that when something does not meet your criteria, you are in the habit of serving prohibition notices." "Only when necessary" I replied. "Well, let us hope that is not the case in my school". Then, with a dismissive gesture of her hand, she said: "Well, carry on".

The last time I had been dismissed in such a fashion was when I was in the army. My trainee said: "Bloody hell. You did well there not to respond to that outburst". I replied: "I took that all on the chin because Sister Mary is the best Head Teacher in the Borough, and in a way, I can see where she is coming from. Remember all this Health and Safety is relatively new".

I carried out the inspection as planned, and sure enough there were a couple of things that were in breach of the new Regulations, so prohibition notices were duly served. I reported back to Sister Mary, informing her that the vast majority of the school was in an excellent condition, but also outlining the two areas of concern. "I knew it!" she replied. "What happens next?" I told her that activities in both areas would have to cease until improvements could be instigated. "I suppose it will be months before these measures are carried out", she replied. I said "I am afraid I cannot give a time factor on that Sister". Her response was: "No of course you can't! You just rock the boat and leave it to others to sort it out! I said I was sorry, and we left.

But I had no intention of leaving it there. Immediately, I contacted two of the local councillors who were on the education committee and put them in the picture, stressing that Sister Mary deserved top priority, and if possible could the remedial measure be carried out within a week, because failure to do so could have an adverse effect on the pending Students' exams. I was very pleased when my request was met within days. On my return visit I was treated by a very different Sister Mary who invited me to sit down and then sent for tea and biscuits. She informed me of the recent conversation she had with one of the councillors involved, who had told her about my intervention and how highly I had spoken of both her and her school.

In nineteen eighty eight, I was given one of the most unusual and unique roles in Health and Safety when, I was put in charge of the Jean Michel Jarre concert that was to be held outdoors in the Royal Victoria Dock. The concert was performed from a floating stage and the spectators were accommodated on tiered seats supported by scaffolding.

On the other side of the dock was the old Spiller's Flour Mill building. All the windows on the dockside wall had been painted white, and the reason for this was that the wall was used as a gigantic screen. So, the wonderful concert began, and in conjunction with the mood music being played, images which complemented the music were projected across the dock onto the screen. During the concert a thunder storm broke out: it was as if God wanted an input because the thunder and lightning was completely sympathetic and in tune with the awe inspiring music being played. Lastly, to top it all I had the best seat in the house.

Over the years, Health and Safety has had a lot of bad press, but I just want to share, with the reader, an incident that happened many years later, when I had become a consultant in this field. The company I was working for ran a large welding shop in Canning Town, and had been successful in getting a very good contract with a large concern, which was renovating a retail complex in Oxford Street in Central London. My job was to present all the necessary paperwork, for example, safety policies, method statements, risk assessments and training procedures. Before the contract was issued, I was invited to a meeting with the safety section of the prime contractor. The meeting was to be held on the site of the renovation. On arrival I was greeted by a security guard, who asked about the reason for my visit, which I duly explained. He then asked if I had the necessary safety clothing, which comprised: a High visibility jacket, hard hat, and toe-tector boots. I said that I had. Then he asked me to put them on, and he inspected them. I asked him if everything was okay, and he said it was, and he was just checking to ensure that the items conformed, which they did. Just as I was going to sign in the visitor's book, he asked me if I could read out loud, the words on the notice board, which indicated the safety rules of the site. Once again I did as he requested. On all of the sites I had previously visited, I had never been so closely vetted. The guard explained that the reason for asking me to read the regulations out loud is that on many London building sites, including this one, there are people from other countries who do not speak English very well. He said that that is why he usually asked them, if they understood what they had just read? "This problem is normally solved by one of their friends, who had a better understanding of the language, and is able to explain it to them" he added. At that point he spoke to someone on his walkie-talkie, informing them of my presence, and I was taken up to the floor where my welders were working.

On the way up I was struck by the tidiness of the site and how everybody was complying with the latest requirements of the Act. At last I got to my gang and asked them how things were going? The charge hand replied: "We thought you were tough on health and safety, John, but this is the tightest site regarding safety we have ever worked on. For instance, every Monday morning, prior to starting work, we have a safety reminder talk and all of our equipment is checked to ensure that it is in good working order. Also, the site safety officer inspects each floor daily". To say I was impressed is to put it mildly. Now, just in case you are thinking this is going overboard a bit, this is what the Managing Director told me when I asked him how his really tight safety regime had paid off on completion of the contract? His reply was as follows: "Along with having an extremely compliant workforce, the contract finished before the estimated date, was below budget and had the lowest accident rate per head of workforce in the country". I have often used this illustration as an example when I get negative responses to Health and Safety, from the various companies for whom I have acted as consultant.

On a lighter note, when working for Newham, one of the areas I covered was an archaeological, tenth century site in Barking. The person in charge was a lovely man called Ken, who was also the Curator of the local museum. On this particular day, his team were down on the site trowelling in a ditch as normal To lighten the situation I had the idea of throwing three coins forged Roman coins, ostensibly from the fourth century, into the area being examined. I said: "Ken, look at these three coins. I am told they are Constantine fourth century, what do you think?" He replied: "No John. I am afraid they are phonies"." Oh!" I said. "If that's the case I might as well get rid of them." So I threw them into the work area without anyone seeing what I had done. Ken started to say something, but I put my finger to my lips and said "Shush, let's see what happens". Ken shook his head but played along, and in no time at all, one of the coins was found. The finder said that it looked like a Constantine coin, from the fourth century, but that that did not make sense. Then the other two were discovered, causing much excitement and debate, until Ken could stand it no longer and told them of my little escapade. With that, they all jumped out of their trench, tools in hand, which just allowed me time to beat a hasty retreat, probably no way for a professional officer of the council to behave! I think what they had in mind, was for me to be found as a relic on a future dig. You can imagine the reception I got on the following day! Ken gave me back my three coins which I still have, and advised me to put them where the sun doesn't shine!

An inspection of a science department in one of the Borough's Comprehensive Schools gave rise to another unforeseen incident. After completing the main area, we were going along one of the main corridors which led to the next room, when I came upon a large cupboard. I said to the teacher that I needed to look inside. He replied that it was okay and just contained some of his personal belongings. I replied: "I am sorry but my brief is to look everywhere except your personal locker". By now he was getting slightly angry, but I insisted, and said: "If you have the key could you please open it up". He replied: "I haven't got it with me but I will get it". Shortly afterwards, he returned and opened it up. His reluctance to open it was not surprising because inside, there were many bottles of chemicals, some of which had been banned for years and others that were unstable and might react violently in certain circumstances. It cost the authority thirteen thousand pounds to dispose of the contents of that cupboard, safely.

I began this chapter by saying that over the years, health and safety had been given a bad press. This has been caused by some people, with little or no experience in the field, banning things for safety reasons that are questionable. For instance, I have read recently that in one school the head teacher wanted to shorten the white stick of a partially blind little girl, on the grounds that other children might trip over it. The stick is a particular length so that there is sufficient time to take evasive action, if the child detects an obstacle by using the stick. Shortening it would increase the possibility of the child colliding with the object they are trying to avoid. It is important to leave risk assessments to those who have proper training and a modicum of common sense.

One of my major inspections was of Stratford Town Hall, a building that was very old, but still had a quality about it. Quite a lot of improvements were needed, but during my tour of the ground floor, I noticed that between the reveals of the large windows and the main side wall, there was a gap of nearly two inches, which meant that the wall was beginning to lean outwards, onto the adjacent pavement. I reported my findings to my boss Ron, immediately. He in turn, brought it to the attention of the powers that be and the Chief Executive sent for me. He asked if I had the necessary knowledge to make this kind of observation and I replied: "I am not a surveyor, but I was a property inspector for the housing department, so I was sufficiently versed in recognising a structural problem when I saw it". He replied: "Thank you, but I still want a second opinion". So a building surveyor also carried out an inspection and his survey tallied exactly with mine. As a result, the building was declared unsafe, which meant all the staff working there had to be relocated.

It was decided that the work undertaken would combine the carrying out of repairs to the wall adjacent to the pavement together with the improvements needed as a result of my inspection. However, whilst some electrical repairs were underway, a fire broke out, causing extensive damage to the whole building. A total of four million pounds was required to carry out all repairs and renovations.

The Education Department had been based in the Town Hall, and the Administrative Head was a very good Christian friend of mine called Barry Sansum. The morning after the fire, my boss asked me to visit to determine if there was anything our department needed to do. On arrival I went to the main office where I found Barry, who is one of the most dedicated officers that I have ever had the privilege to meet. When he saw this beautiful old building so badly damaged, it really got to him. Being Christian brothers it seemed only right that we should join in prayer to lessen his sorrow. Some forty years later, Barry still remembers that prayer time. On completion of the renovations a small celebration party was held, and it has to be said that the building really had been restored to its original grandeur.

On my initial inspection of the building, I found a very old and dilapidated throne like chair in the basement area. I told Barry about and asked if I could buy it. He had a look at it and decided it would have been put in the rubbish skip anyway, so he said that ten pounds seemed a reasonable price. I loaded the chair onto the back seat of my car, a very satisfied customer. I spent the next number of weekends renovating the chair, until I thought it was worthy of going onto the altar of the Mayflower Chapel. When it was finally in position, I was well pleased. But, somehow Jack Hart, who was one of the Aldermen of the Borough, heard about my purchase. He contacted Barry and asked if he realised that the chair he had sold to me was the old West Ham Mayoral Seat, and that they had been looking for it for years. So, in turn Barry contacted me and said: "Sorry John, but it has got to be returned". I did so and he gave me back my tenner. When he saw the restored condition of the chair he said: "I am so sorry John, but as a consolation I am sure Jack Hart would like me to thank you". I gave a shrug and said: "Some you win, some you lose".

In total I was employed by Newham Council for twenty three years and I have very fond memories of my time there. The great and close friendships made still exist, and have been both enjoyable and informative. But for one reason or another I decided to move on. When I had announced my intention of leaving, I was sent for by the now promoted Chief Executive, Barry Sansum, who asked me to stay. I explained that all was not well between Ron, my boss and I, and it would be better for all concerned if I left. So, with very real reluctance I took voluntary redundancy.

Thirty-Four: Sporting Times

I am a firm believer that if you want to keep your mind working well, then it must be coupled with keeping the rest of the body in good shape. Since my army days, I have carried out a fairly strict regime involving weight lifting, running, boxing training, and swimming, and hopefully, without sounding boastful, still manage to carry out three, three hour sessions a week at my local gym in Harold Hill, at the age of eighty. Around the early eighties, I was carrying out a lot of my track work at the Terry McMillan stadium in Newham: this was coupled with road work to increase my stamina. I remember coming home one evening from the track, when my wife Brenda, said: "I was thinking about doing a bit of keep fit myself, but there is no way I would do road work. I would be too embarrassed". I gave our conversation a lot of thought and came to the conclusion that there must be a lot of people like Brenda who wanted a bit of privacy at first, in getting fit. So with this thought in mind, my first port of call was to a very good friend of mine, Shirley Miller, who at that time was the Head of Newham's Leisure Services. Part of her remit was the running of the stadium. I put it to her that, if she would allow me to use the track on Tuesday and Thursday evenings, it might benefit a lot of presently unfit people, in Newham. I also told her about the conversation I had had with my wife which had informed my thinking. She agreed in principle, but said she would have to get committee approval, especially as I wanted it rent free. Also, she wanted a method statement from me, giving details of the practical way I intended to make this idea a reality. As well as contacting, Shirley I got in touch with the Head of Newham's Health Authority and had a meeting with her, once again explaining my plan. Her response was very positive and she began asking if I had any experience in the field of getting fit, and if I would consider overseeing ways of combatting obesity. I replied: "If you are thinking about dieting and exercise I can think of no better way of achieving reasonable goals in that direction". In answer to her question regarding experience I told her about my coaching qualification in weight training and body building, which was coupled with health and safety knowledge and experience and many years of track and road work. As an illustration of risk assessment, I said: "If someone came to me in the stadium and they appeared obviously overweight, the first thing I would do is to ask them to walk around the track in their own time. Then I would ask if they had any medical conditions. If they had, I would say that I would definitely like them to try to lose weight and get fit, but I would need medical approval first. This would involve getting a letter from their doctor to confirm that they were able to participate in the team's activities."

The Head of that Department seemed to like my answer and promised to back me to the hilt, also saying that her clinic would help on a personal basis if I thought it was appropriate. I am sorry about name dropping, but the editor of the Newham Recorder, Tom Duncan, was a mate of mine. He too, saw where I was coming from, and said: "Okay Johnny. As soon as Shirley gives you the go ahead, I will give you a spot in the Paper". Within two weeks, Shirley gave me the nod of approval, so back to Tom I went. He really did me proud. The headline read 'Hope for Embarrassed Joggers', and went on to explain the venue, times and the principle of what I had in mind for anyone who was interested.

The First Tuesday evening arrived and over eighty people turned up. I couldn't believe that so many people thought along the same lines as my Brenda. I assembled them all in the large hall of the adjacent school, which I had also been successful in getting as a free let. Then I introduced myself and gave them a set of gentle warm up exercises. I had a good look at what they were wearing, and where needed, gave advice on suitable footwear and clothing. Finally, we all went onto the track, where to my surprise the photographer from the Recorder was waiting. I have still got a great shot of some of us on that first night, and again, Tom the editor gave the club another lovely spread the following week. After everyone had walked a few laps of the track, we returned back to the hall for a warm down, and a pep talk. The essence of this was that since most of them had been very unfit over many years, they should not expect to run marathons in a few weeks. But I said that I could promise them that if they all stuck with it, they would, if needed, lose weight and certainly would feel and look a lot better. On the second week one of our friends named Helen come to join us.

Following the format of the first week, I asked her and her friend to walk the track, so that I could assess them. When she had completed her lap I beckoned her over, and said: "Helen, I told you to walk the track." She turned to her friend and said: "I did, didn't I?" "That's right. You did." I replied. "But what I did not tell you to do was to have a fag on the back stretch!" She laughed and said: "Sorry John. I didn't think you could see me from there". What really pleased me was the cross section of ages, the youngest eleven and the oldest nearly seventy, of both sexes.

One evening a Mum called Janet, brought her son, Kenny to the track. Kenny had some learning difficulties and was quite introverted. Janet asked if she and Kenny could join our club, which by now was officially called the Newham Joggers. I said that of course they could join and they were both very welcome. Although Kenny may have found difficulties in some areas, endurance and speed were not amongst them. In no time at all he was showing many of us a clean pair of heels. Christmas came and we celebrated our first year as a club with a brilliant party, and when I announced Kenny as the "Man of Year" there was wild applause and approval. Kenny was and is still a lovely fella, who is no longer the shy young man who first came to our club, but instead has run many marathons all over the world, which makes both me and his Mum Janet, very proud people.

Over the years, the members and I ran many marathons in various places over our part of the country, but one of the most popular runs was the Sunday Times Newspaper two and a half miler. This was held in Hyde Park, once a year on a Sunday. Thousands took part. The runs were broken up into age groups, starting with the twenty to thirty, and so on, until there were some very elderly folk in their seventies to eighties giving it a go.

The last run was a collective one of all age groups and it really was a sight to behold. Our club was assembled quite close to the finishing line and we were determined not to leave before the final person had crossed the line. That very last person was a very disabled young boy of about ten years old. His little feet were barely touching the ground, and the rest of his body was lovingly cradled by his Dad. I have got to tell you that I have never heard cheers so loud, and an outpouring of such love and encouragement in all my life, most of us were in tears.

At that time, along with quite a few members of the club, I ran a good number of half marathons, but could never manage a full twenty-six miles as my right knee would give out, which was a real disappointment.

However sitting round our table at Christmas time with my three sons, one of them said: "What are you going to do to celebrate your fiftieth birthday Dad? It was in January, and I had been toying with this idea for a while, so I answered: "The London Triathlon." "Are you sure dad?" they collectively replied. "That's a tough one." I replied: "Yep. I am going to give it my best shot". So began a very strict regime of training, which involved running, cycling and swimming. The swimming raised a few eyebrows especially when it was in the Royal Victoria Dock which is the venue used for the event. I had to get clearance from the Port of London Authority for me to do this. I began training in late June and the water was still very cold, so as a preventative measure against hypothermia and drowning, I asked Brenda to accompany me. Her job was to trail a length of rope over the side of the quay wall, so if I did get into trouble, she could pull me along to one of the quayside ladders. So, I began keeping close to the side, and every now and then I would catch sight of the rope, but no Brenda. Eventually I called out loudly: "Brenda where are you?" A distant voice replied: "Over here". I answered: "That's no good mate. If I get into trouble you won't be able to see me". She replied. "I can't help that John, but you know I'm frightened of deep water". Well that was her excuse, but I think she had a hidden agenda! What do you reckon?

The reader will probably remember that this was the same dock into which my dad had ridden his bike. Also, if you did fall in, it meant twenty four-hours in hospital, in quarantine. The water had been tested and clearance given, but the sight of me swimming in it still raised a few eyebrows, especially amongst the old dockworkers. The day of the event dawned and the mile swim was the first part. Today, the athletes wear tri-suits, and underneath is the cycling/running gear. We just had normal swimming costumes, and the changing facilities were nil: it was just in an old warehouse at the end of the swim. As I clambered out, next to me was a woman of about my age. Seeing there was nowhere we could modestly change, I said: "Sorry darling, but time is not on our side." She agreed that this was no time for modesty, so we stripped off and changed. Unbeknown to me, my son Steve was watching from the entrance, and on seeing our striptease, called out, "Mum the old man is stripping off with a bird in here! Troublemaker! I managed to complete the Triathlon in three hours fifty seven minutes, and was well pleased, since my aim was to have finished in under four hours.

I ran the jogging club for nearly five years, but by then it had become naturally more elite. Many of the members had progressed to good distance runners and the Newham Joggers, which was its second title, was no longer suitable. So, with some reluctance I left the club and handed it over to new management. It was then renamed the East London Road Runners, which I believe still exists and is highly respected. The saying 'from little acorns…' spring to mind!

In both 2000 and 2001, I was part of a team from the Peacock Gym that rowed in a Montague Whaler, twenty-two miles along the Thames from Richmond to Millwall. On each occasion it took just under four and half hours to complete. This is an annual event and it is called the Great River Race. It's a wonderful sight to behold, with over three hundred crafts, of all shapes and sizes, taking part.

I get a great kick as I am driving along the Thames Embankment knowing that I and the brilliant boys from the Peacock Gym have rowed under every bridge this side of the Dartford crossing. I was the oldest member of the team, and to this day it remains one of the most enjoyable but toughest ventures, in which I have ever been involved.

I was aged about eleven when I had my first introduction to boxing. This was when a travelling fair made its annual visit to Becton Road Park, and part of its attraction was a boxing booth. At around seven pm, the time at which the local men would get home from work, the man who ran the booth would begin using a trumpet shaped haler to challenge the locals to see if they could last three rounds with any of his fighters. It was not usually a problem, because in and around Custom House there were many young fellas who were useful with their fists. Now, the men of these booths were amongst the toughest and fittest you could find in any sport. They fought at least once a night a twice on Saturdays, once in the afternoon and then again in the evening. There was not an ounce of surplus fat on any of them. Each of the three rounds lasted three minutes, so in the mind of a lay person who has little knowledge of boxing, especially if they had supped a few pints, nine minutes should be manageable. If they voiced this to their mates, you can bet your bottom dollar that one of them would have called out to the booth owner, "Oi mate my mucker here will step up to the mark". This put the potential challenger on the spot, but with the rest of his mates now urging him on, up he would feel obliged to go, to the front.

Normally the booth had three fighters, and the owner would pick one of these who were around the same weight as the now pretty apprehensive looking challenger. Practically every one of these fights took on the same pattern. The challenger would fly out of the corner with fists banging out in every direction. However, nobody can keep this up for any length of time without flagging. But the pro fighter would give him a chance to recover, by boxing on the back foot for a while. This would be designed to have a three-fold effect. It would prevent the challenger from losing face; he would last at least one round; and lastly and importantly for business, it would not act as a too much of a deterrent to other young men who fancied their chances.

Every now and then one of our local boxers would take up the challenge. One of these was a young fella from Jersey Road called Billy Mann. This time it was a whole different ball game. Billy was on par with the booth fighter and fought a terrific bout, in which he went the full three rounds. The booth manager got into the ring, gave Billy his reward and said: "You were lucky tonight, but I bet you couldn't do that again". Billy replied: "Give me two days and I will be back".

In the interim, word had travelled about this oncoming fight and on the night when Billy made his return, the booth was totally full. Again, he held his own and went the distance, to massive applause. Many of those in attendance, me included, reckon he just about won. In later life, as I reflect on this event, I realise how clever that booth owner was at turning over a few quid.

Boxing booths and the associated types of fights and boxers have a history of over two hundred years, and many champions came from this background. One in particular, who was one of my heroes, was Randolph Turpin. He had two epic fights with another brilliant and charismatic fighter called Sugar Ray Robinson.

I was never very competitive in sports as a youngster, except I did like boxing. So, I joined the Canning Town Docklands Settlement Club, to learn about the 'noble art' of self-defence'. At the club I gained sufficient skills to be picked for Shipman Road Schools' Boxing Team, and during one of our practice matches held in the school, I found my opponent was a good mate, and still is, named Teddy Demmon. I figured I stood a good chance against him, and with that in mind, I invited a young girl I fancied along to the match to show my prowess. It did not go according to plan. Teddy had developed a beautiful straight left, which totally disturbed the carefully coiffured quiff in the front of my hair. Needless to say, once my limited looks had been shattered, the young girl I admired was not impressed.

All the schools in West Ham had their own boxing teams, and at that time, West Ham had a reputation of producing very fine boxers. A few of the schoolboys competing at that time, went onto become Great Britain champions, and both Teddy and I won a number of contests. Teddy went further than I did, perhaps because I was unfortunate enough to meet two of the potential champions, fairly early on in the preliminaries.

One time, I cut the base of my thumb during a woodwork lesson and it required stitches. This could not have happened at a worse time, because an interschool fight was due, which rather foolishly, I made up my mind, that I was not going to miss. Of course, my injured hand was heavily bandaged, so to allay any suspicion I bandaged up the other one. When I was being gloved up, the teacher asked about the bandages. I said that I had seen pictures of boxers doing this to protect their knuckles, so I thought I would give it a try. The teacher, who was not our normal trainer, had just been brought in to give a helping hand. He just shrugged his shoulders and put my gloves on. Unfortunately, during the second round I miss-punched and knocked my injured thumb back. I immediately felt the tear as the stiches broke and my glove felt wet as the blood began to leak. I managed to complete the fight, but then came the time to remove my gloves. Straightaway my foolhardiness was apparent. My trainer was summoned and was furious at my deception.

I was sent back to the hospital to have the stitches re-done and the dressing reapplied. The next day, back in school, I was sent for by the Head Master. I could see he was not well pleased. He asked me about my other hand, and I said it was fine. He replied: "Good. Now hold it out with your palm uppermost." With that, he gave me two of the best with his trusty, thin bamboo cane. Then he said: "That was a very stupid and dangerous thing to do. Do you agree?" Without waiting for a reply he said: "Now get back to your class". But, just as I was leaving, he said: "By the way, did you win?" "Yes Sir." I replied. "Good! Now, off you go."

The next time I boxed was in Wellington, New Zealand when I was a Merchant seaman. A local vicar had the idea of getting a match together between local boxers and visiting sailors. He came on board to make enquiries and one of the fellas, said: "Johnny Ringwood has done a bit." He came to find me and we agreed that I would give it a go. He then asked me to go to the local gym, to assess whether or not I was up to it. I was matched with a guy who was a novice, so it was not too hard to impress. The bout was arranged shortly after and was held in a fairly small hall. It was attended by a good number of Kiwis and crew members of visiting boats, and I was appearing in the third bout of the programme. I looked across the ring and saw that my opponent was a good bit bigger than me. I also recognised him from my visit to the gym and remembered his well-worn boxing boots, always a good sign of a seasoned fighter, who knows the score. We were called to the centre of the ring and our names were read out. It was announced that this was a catch-weight contest, which explained why he was heavier than me. I was totally unfit through smoking, boozing and so on, and should not have been allowed in the front row, let alone the ring.

I figured I had just one good round in me, so at the sound of the bell I went out all guns firing. I might as well have hit him with a powder puff for all the effect it had, but then he started to talk to me in a very sarcastic way, saying: "Ouch that hurt!", and "Oh I am going to watch you!" As I tried an upper cut he said: "Come on mate, you are going to have to do better that that". I survived the first round just about, and went out to try to even it up a bit, but to no avail. Then he said: "Have you had enough yet mate? I have." With that he hit me with a devastating left hook, which spun me like a top and down I went. I remember it was like a Walt Disney film. There were bright lights, stars and planets zooming around in my head, and on the count of five, I started to come round to find my second, who was my crewmate named Peter, bending over me. He said: "Stay where you are John". I replied: "Too bloody right", and was counted out. On getting out of the ring, the vicar said: "Well done!" I replied: "Yeah you're right there, I bleeding well was!" Especially, since it turned out that my opponent was the local champion at his weight.

I may not have been anything to write home about regarding my boxing skills, but my brother Jimmy was a good fighter. He was a member of the famous West Ham Boxing Club and he was very skilled indeed. On one occasion, his opponent was an Irish champion, and he arrived in the ring wearing an emerald green dressing gown adorned with shamrocks, Jimmy's sartorial dress consisted of a vest with a hole in it, shorts and a pair of black canvas slippers. Round one showed that the Irish kid was certainly good, but Jimmy was finding his weak spots and landing some good sharp shots. My brother was very fit and came back to the corner barely blowing. I was leaning on the cuff of the apron and said to him "You alright mate?" He replied: "Yeah, he's going this round." Sure enough, with a short, sharp punch to the solar plexus, the other guy folded. I said to Jimmy: "How did you know you were going to do him in the second?" He replied: "I noticed he was a bit puffy round the middle and winced every time I hit him there, even with light shots. So I knew if I really whacked him there, he would go, and sure enough he did."

Jimmy could have turned professional. He certainly had the ability, but alcohol took its toll and finished any ambitions in that direction. I lost my little brother at the very early age of forty nine, a talent wasted in so many areas.

Still, even at my age I can hold my own in our local gym on the punch bag, doing three, three minute hard hitting rounds. Sometimes, out of the corner of my eye, I catch sight of a youngster, watching my session. I imagine he's thinking to himself, if that old boy can do it, it can't be that hard, so he dons gym gloves and has a crack, but within about thirty seconds, he is puffing and blowing. I always speak to the kid, asking if he is okay and would like to improve his skill and stamina. If he says he would, then I show him the rudiments of boxing and how to pace himself. I have to confess that this has backfired somewhat, because now I have to wait my turn to get on the bag.

Thirty-Five: New Pastures

On leaving Newham Council, I was fortunate enough to get a position as a health and safety manager with a Security company who were subcontracted to the London Docklands Development Corporation known as the LDDC. This appointment was really a new kettle of fish. Whilst at the Council, my handwritten reports had been dealt with by the typing department, this was the new age of personal computers and I was informed that, in future, my new company expected me to present my health and safety paper work in typewritten form. I informed Tom, my manager that I didn't have a clue with regards to computers, so I was sent on a half-day's course to get acquainted with new technology. I remember the teacher saying: "Now hit the return button, but not so hard John. They are complaining about the noise downstairs". Also there was no Mike or Helen to cover the areas they had been responsible for: there was just little old me.

Not only did I have to carry out duties with the LDDC, but I was also responsible for the health and safety of our own company's staff, which meant carrying out inspections all over London and the surrounding areas.

My new role was varied and interesting. One aspect of this was the frequent use of the docks and related buildings for filming and television series, and my role was to work in conjunction with the H&S sections of these different organisations. At times this was a tad difficult, especially when the building being used was in a very poor state of repair. In the minds of the directors in charge of filming, this was often exactly what the script required, with the shabbiness echoing the tone of the subject and production. Sometimes that left me very little room for manoeuvre, but somehow, with a common sense attitude and donning my drama hat, instead of my usual hard one, allowable compromises were made.

In time, we moved out of the main LDDC building and were re-sited to the historical Trinity Buoy Wharf, which was a fabulous site for an ex-sea dog like me because the wharf was on the river Thames. After a while, it also became the venue for artists. Some of the works were beyond my comprehension, but others were easily identifiable and spectacular, in some cases. During my lunch hour, I would often wander to where the artists were working, and on one occasion I was looking at a framed piece of work, which appeared to be just a horizontal straight line. The artist who was nearby, saw my puzzled look, and asked me what I thought of it. I said: "I am sorry, but it just looks like a line to me." Then he produced a very strong magnifying glass and said: "Now have another look." I did so, and to my astonishment, a number of human figures in different poses, were depicted within that line. I shook his hand and said: "Brilliant!"

On another occasion, one of the artists had made a trumpet- like tube of plaster, which began from the inside of a window and then projected some eight feet onto the outside ground area. It was very narrow at the window end, but increased in circumference at the far end. It took about a week to complete. I passed it on my way to lunch, but on my return it was in pieces, and I was told that the artist had smashed it up. The next morning Tom, my boss told me to inspect the outside areas to ensure everything was in good order, as the LDDC bosses were making a visit. I told him about the plaster work and he said: "Get rid of it". So one of the boys got hold of a wheel barrow into which the remains of the cone were loaded for disposal. As I was passing the now cleared site, I found the artist screaming at one the fellas who helped me clear it. I asked: "What was the problem?" He replied: "You! You are the problem! Where is my art work?" I replied: "What art work? It was just a pile of smashed up plaster". He roared: "You philistine! That broken plaster represented all my anger and pent up feelings, and I want you dealt with!" I replied: Well, not being an artist, I cannot really see your reasoning, but if you want to report me then you had better come and see my boss". So then the two of us proceeded to Tom's office. I don't normally criticise anyone's appearance, but this guy did look a bit strange. His hair was tied in a knot on the front of his head, and he had another knot in his beard on his chin. Without bothering to knock, he barged into Tom's office with me trailing behind. Tom was not amused with this intrusion, but with a calm, soft voice that belied his temper, he asked: "Can I help you?" The knotted one began ranting about the reasons for the smashed plaster, saying that in his view it was a work of art, which had been destroyed, by me, and again called me a philistine. Tom replied:

"I am sorry you have taken this point of view, but in the absence of your artistic interpretation and knowledge, I can only concur with John's actions. Also, you had not given any indication that the plaster pieces should not be disturbed, so I have decided this matter can go no further. My officer was just carrying out my instructions regarding clearing up the outside areas". Then Tom asked me if I had anything else to add? I replied: "If it helps, just to say that the mood of the plaster in the skip looked pretty angry." As you might have guessed this was not appreciated by old Knotty, who screamed: "That's not funny and I intend to take this further." With that, off he flounced.

During my time with this Company I met a great guy called Alistair. He was an ex-army captain, straight out of the top draw with an accent to match. But, now his role was the company training officer. We hit it off straight away. I think it was his wicked sense of humour that appealed to me most. One day he asked me if I had ever gone horse racing. I said that I hadn't, and then he asked if I would like to go. I said that I would and that it was something I had often thought about. Alistair went on to say that his old regiment has a military day at Sandown race course, and that all the jockeys are serving soldiers. Being an old soldier, that certainly appealed to me. So, on the appointed day, off to Sandown we went. On arriving Alistair introduced me to his lovely and charming wife Tory. I am afraid we spent as much time at the bar as we did at the racing area, and of course, because of my lack of knowledge, when I did have a bet I didn't have a lot of luck.

After the racing had finished, everyone went back to the carpark. The car boots were opened revealing very well stocked hampers as well as a plentiful supply of top quality wines and spirits. And I really did appreciate Tory's mother taking me under her wing, seeing as I was a little out of my comfort zone. One of the gentlemen in the assembled company said "I have just noticed your tie. If I am not wrong I believe it's that of the Royal Fusiliers Regiment. Am I right?" I replied: "Spot on. That was my old regiment." "He said: "Well, there's a coincidence, it was also mine. I served as the Colonel of the Regiment for a number of years. " He asked me when I served and what was my rank? I replied that I served as a National Serviceman from 1957-1959, and just as a Fusilier. He replied very graciously, that there was no-one in our regiment who was 'just' a fusilier. Every man who served, no matter what rank, was considered very special. It turned out that amongst those assembled were three other Colonels, as well as my Fusilier's comrade. I went with Alistair to Sandown over the following years, and every one of those trips was very, very special. Needless to say, my wardrobe was increased, accordingly, with tweeds and trilbies.

I have a lot for which to thank this employer, because working there widened my knowledge of the world outside local government, in which I had served for so long. Also, it made me also appreciate how tough and competitive the commercial world can be. The contract with LDDC was coming to a close and although there would have been a post for me at the head office, I declined. So, once again I chose to step into the unknown.

Thirty-six:
The Big Step

My wife Brenda has always been my rock, and this was her advice: "John, why work for anyone else. You have loads of knowledge now, so why not take the big plunge and work for yourself". As always, I considered her advice to be good. I agreed and decided to go the whole hog. I called my new venture JCR Health and Safety Consultancy Limited. Now, anyone who has travelled this route knows that it's far easier said than done. The first thing was to notify the appropriate authorities of my intention and get registered. Then I had to get an accountant and insurance cover. Within six weeks and with the necessary approval, I was set to go. Already, I had many contacts in my field of work, so along with them and advertising, jobs started to come in.

I worked from home, initially, which was fine if I was just carrying out inspections, audits and surveys, but, I had other ideas which involved training, and this included First Aid courses. For many years I had been a practising first aider, but now I wanted to become a trainer. This was accomplished by attending a twelve week course run by the St John Ambulance Brigade. I was fortunate enough to pass both the written and practical exams and could now embark on training others.

Tony and Martin Bowers are two of the finest gentlemen/ rascals, I have ever had the pleasure to meet. I got to know them during my time with the Council, having inspected one of their gyms, which was in a classroom of one of the Borough's schools. I was impressed then, by their dedication to the local people of all ages. But a few years passed and these two friends had progressed to owning and running the world renowned Peacock Boxing Gym in Canning Town. I trained there, and during one of my sessions I got talking to Martin about looking for a training room, when to my surprise, he said "I think we have got exactly what you want". With that he took me to a room on the top floor, which appeared to be ideal, but needed to be furnished. Fortunately, next door to the Peacock, was a place owned by another friend who dealt in second hand office furniture. With the combined resources of both of these friends I was soon ready to go. I could not believe my luck at how things were falling into place.

Now, of course, I needed some clients. This was achieved, when organisations answered my advertisements and securing a major contract from Newham Council. In a comparatively short time I was running four day first aid classes for up to thirty people at a time. Those attending loved the place. It certainly had an atmosphere all of its own. I recollect one occasion on which one of the young boxers came out of the changing rooms with just with a towel wrapped around his midriff. At the time I was talking to one of the young woman on the course, when I noticed her eyes had drifted towards the young towel-wrapped athlete. To get her attention back, I enquired: "Young lady, are you listening to me?" She replied quietly: "No John. I am studying anatomy."

I had really landed on my feet, because I would arrive at the gym at six am, have two half hour training sessions, shower, change and then ready for the day. What a life!

Over the next few years I got contracts with other London Boroughs, who required both First Aid and Health and Safety training. During that time I successfully trained over five thousand people on how to heal a hurt and possibly save a life. For the life of me, I cannot think of a better legacy.

I was often asked how to get fit in questions from course members who knew of my background. I always replied that in most cases, people think that it is a quick remedy, but in reality, it's a long term thing. To illustrate the point and determine their level of fitness I would take their blood pressure and if they were obviously overweight, advise them to diet. On one occasion I took the blood pressure of a middle-aged woman who was certainly not overweight, and I was alarmed by how very high both readings were. During the lunch break I spoke to her quietly, and advised her to go to her doctor's that evening, just for a check-up. She failed to attend the rest of the course. A few weeks later I received a telephone call from her. She said that she wanted to thank me because according to her doctor, there was a very strong chance that if treatment had not been given, she would have suffered a stroke or a heart attack. The same lady returned on a later course, which she completed successfully.

On another occasion, I had a very mischievous young black lady, on one of my first aid courses, who liked to be called Sexy Mel. All through the next four days she kept us amused with her antics, but on one occasion when she was moving one of the other members of the course into the recovery position, she really went overboard, rolling her eyes and looking at the casualty, longingly. She happened to be wearing a very tight pair of lycra trousers, and just for a second I lost it, and gave her a sharp smack on her backside and told her: "Mel behave yourself". There was a stunned silence from the rest of the course who were all Council employees, and I thought to myself, 'that's it Johnny boy, now you have blown it'. But good old Mel said: "Ooh that was nice John. Do it again". Whew, I have never been so relieved.

As well as full four day courses, I used to run a course for one day, which meant I would travel all over London carrying them out, but the places that will always stick in my mind were when I taught the staff of schools for children with special needs: I have never witnessed so much care and love being shown. My heart would be lifted and melted simultaneously, especially at Christmas time when these very special children would sing and entertain us.

The great thing about working for one's self is the satisfaction of seeing the business grow and that all the hard work and sacrifices made suddenly appear to be paying off. I have mentioned before that I am a people person and this new role totally embraced that concept.

The clients on one of my one day First Aid classes consisted of young fellas around the age of seventeen and eighteen who were unemployed, so the first-aid training was part of a scheme put in place for them to get some work experience. Their main course was about gardening, most of them were attentive to the first-aid information except one. I knew straight away that he was going to give me some hassle. His whole attitude was negative. He lounged about with his feet on the chair in front, looking out of the windows, and yawning loudly. I asked him if he was interested in learning first-aid. He answered: "Nah. Not really. It's a load of old crap as far as I am concerned. I have only come on this course because I was told to." I was not going to let him get away with this. I could have chucked him off the course, but Mrs Abercrombie came to mind, and I felt compelled to give him a second chance. So I replied: "Okay son. We need to talk." So, at lunch break we had a conversation. This is how it went. I asked him why he was giving me a rough ride? He answered "Cos that's the way I am." I said: "What are you, a tough guy?" "Tougher than you", was his response. I asked if he would like to prove it and he asked how that would be done. "Down stairs in the ring", I answered. Obviously, not wishing to lose face, he replied: "Yeah Okay". As we were going down the stairs, I bumped into my personal trainer, Eddie, who asked how things were going. I replied that I was going to have some lunch in a while, but that first of all, this young man and I were going to have a workout in the ring. Eddie looked at my companion and said: "Good luck mate, you are going to need it." Before going into the gym, I said to him calling him by his first name, "I want you to listen very carefully to what I am going to say now. I am over seventy years old but I am telling you that without a shadow of a doubt, I am going to get the better of you in that ring, and because, at the moment the gym is very busy, many people will witness it, and with that kind of result your street cred will go straight down to zero. Is that really how you want to play it? At the moment nobody except you, me and Eddie know of our intentions. All you need to do to resolve the problem, is to behave yourself, show me a bit of respect, and maybe even learn a useful skill on the side". I think what Eddie had said sowed a seed of doubt in his mind, because without looking at me, he finally answered "Okay then. Let's leave it there". I answered, "Good. Now let's go and get something to eat."

Totally unprofessional, perhaps, but this is Canning Town and it worked. You see, both this young man and I came out of the same stable. He knew the script, which is that you do not mug someone off, especially in front of others, without expecting a come-back. In case you are wondering why I was pretty confident about having the edge over this young man in the ring, even at seventy years old I was still very fit, and because my training was in the Peacock, quite a lot of it involved boxing training. Although I never actually boxed or sparred at the time, I did carry out all other aspects of the sport. Just a couple of weeks before this little instance, I had been on the pads with Eddie for eight three minute rounds, I even managed to have a go on the pads with Jimmy Tibbs, a world famous trainer of champions.

Thirty-Seven:
After Dinner Speaker!

For one reason or another I was asked to become Chair of the East London Business Association. This happened during our annual dinner which was held in the banqueting suite in the West Ham Football Club. Just before the beginning of the meal one of the administrators approached our table and asked me if I would say a few words. I thought she meant along the lines of an introductory 'welcome to the meeting', so I said that would not be a problem. A short while after, her manager came over and said: "Johnny, you really are a diamond to get us out of this." I replied: "I am a bit lost now. What do you mean?" she answered: "Well, you have agreed to be the after dinner speaker because Tony Banks, (the local MP at the time) cannot make it". "Well, I'll do my best" I replied. One of the fellas on the table asked me what I was going to talk about and I said that I hadn't a clue and was just going to play it by ear.

I began my speech by recalling my time spent in an office in Lime Street, which was a link road between Fenchurch and Leadenhall Streets, and how many East Enders like me had taken this route to find work. But now, because of Canary Wharf and all the other developments that are taking place, the route has reversed and the West End was coming to us. I suggested that it was now our time, but we must be geared up to meet the challenge. That may mean employing more staff to meet the extra needs. I then told them the story about Mrs Abercrombie and how she had changed my whole life by looking beyond the first image presented, and that was my advice to all those who attended and who were potential employers. Then for some unknown reason, I got a standing ovation.

About six months later, I got a telephone call from the President of the UK Architects and Surveyors Institute, who asked me if I could carry out a similar talk at their annual dinner. I asked if there would be a payment He replied: "Yes, four hundred pounds." "That seems very reasonable" I replied So, on the night of the dinner I gave my speech, after which the President came over and said: "Which charity do you want the four hundred pounds to go to?" I am not normally lost for words but I replied: "Charity?" He replied: "Oh yes. Perhaps I didn't explain clearly that all proceeds from this dinner go to charity. But you do receive a whisky decanter and two glasses, along with a fountain pen all marked with the West Ham Football Cub emblem". "Thank you very much", I answered somewhat meekly, not quite knowing what to say. I am still not sure if I had been suckered, but that special night out I had promised Brenda on the proceeds, had to be put on the back burner, for the time being.

Thirty-Eight:
Nearly lost the Peacock

In around the year two thousand, Martin Bowers called me over and said: "I have got some bad news for you Johnny. I think we may have to close the Gym." "Why?" I replied in alarm. Martin replied that he had had a phone call from the man who owned the building. He said that he had seen the television and newspaper stories about the Gym's activities and he reckoned that with all this success, it was time for a rent increase. He proposed to treble the present rent. Martin said they could not afford that, so it meant I would need to start looking around for another venue for my training. However, what the owner of the building had not realised was that the Peacock received so much publicity because of all the voluntary community work that Tony and Martin had carried out. This involved a number football teams, drama, marathon training, outdoor pursuits, Karate, singing and dancing lessons as well as the normal Gym activities. The gym fees were, and still are amongst the cheapest in London. At that time, I was a member of the Canning Town Partnership, the members of which consisted of a number of local people and Councillors for the area. On the way home I thought that there was no way that this vital commodity was going to go to the wall. So, the next morning I said to Martin: "I want you to go to everyone you know and get letters of support outlining all of the community activities that you and your volunteers offer from the Peacock, and in turn, how cost effective those activities are to the youngsters involved, who otherwise could be roaming the streets and maybe getting up to mischief". This was not a hard task for Martin, because the local people were lining up to show their support, both bodily and in writing. So, armed with a stack of letters, I attended the next meeting of the Partnership, and presented the case for the Peacockt. After a fairly short discussion and because everyone knew of the Gym and its reputation, it was agreed, in principle, that the closure of the Peacock should not happen. However, this was not rubber stamped. In fact, every angle of the validity of the gym was examined. Finally a meeting was held with all concerned and sufficient funds, in the form of a grant, was made by the partnership, to buy the lease. This, in turn, was taken over by Newham Council. The final, very happy outcome was that the rent to the Council from the Peacock, was of a peppercorn nature.

Thirty-Nine:
Still Learning

Another of my jobs was in a college in Walthamstow, and one day, the Principal sent for me. He said: "John, although I appreciate you are very well qualified, under the new Ofsted Regulations, if I am going to employ you as a contractor in the future, you will need a Certificate of Education". I asked how I would get this certification and he explained that it could be achieved by attending a one day a week course for a year. Now, so very late in life, I found that once again I was back in college to further my career. It was not easy, for as well as studying I was now running a full time business. But I am pleased to say that at the end of the year, I passed with marks that put me at the top of the class.

Forty:
Calling it a Day

I ran my consultancy for nearly ten years and I can honestly say that without a doubt, they were the happiest and most rewarding times of my working life. There is no greater satisfaction than seeing all that hard work and studying come to fruition. At the age of seventy one, I was teaching on one of my four day, first- aid courses, which was by its nature a very repetitive activity, and suddenly I realised I felt bored. The thought struck me that if I am bored, perhaps that is that having a negative effect on my course members, something I would not want to happen. During the evening I discussed this with Brenda, and as always she gave me the correct answer. She said: "John, you know better than anyone about giving your best, so if that is how you felt today, you are under par, so for all concerned I think now is the time to throw in the towel and retire". All the boys down at the Gym thought I was crazy to pack in such a good business, but as usual, Brenda was right.

Forty-One:
Footlights Beckoned

There was a member on one of my very last courses at the Peacock, who was a barman at the famous Brick Lane Music Hall. I remember him as quite a character. I have to say that all my life I have held a secret ambition to tread the boards, and I shared this with this fella. His reply was: "It's never too late. Why don't you come along to one of our shows and I will introduce you to Vincent Hayes who is the owner". I agreed to this and along I went. It was a great show. Even as a young kid I have always enjoyed old time music hall entertainment, and remember sitting up in the gods of the old Queens Theatre in Poplar, now long gone. After the show I met Vincent who was not only the owner, but also the star of the show, and over a few jars we discussed my hidden dreams. The outcome was that I hired the theatre for a night and put together a show of my own. My family thought that I was having a relapse in my mental condition, but I was deadly serious about having a go. So serious was I, that the first thing I did was to have singing lessons from a lady who was giving lessons to my granddaughter, Georgia, who has a very fine voice. I had lessons for a few months, until my teacher said "You will never be a star, but on the other hand you are good enough for a one night stand". The first half of the show consisted of songs from the First World War. My role was that of Sergeant Tommy Atkins, and I hired an original First World War army uniform from the Kenneth More Theatre. Both my singing teacher and Georgia were also part of the cast. The second half consisted of a sing along. We were accompanied by a good friend of mine who played a very mean guitar, and he was joined by the resident pianist who was superb. After the show, Vincent said that he thought we had done very well, although he didn't offer me a job! In general, his words of comfort were echoed by all those who attended. That was it then, mission accomplished, another patch in my life's quilt.

Forty-Two:
The Dockers' Statue

It was again in the year two thousand, that my wife Brenda, who was at that time working in the office of a local supermarket, came home one night, with the news that an outing had been arranged for a weekend away. It involved visiting the sites of the television programmes called 'The Last of the Summer Wine' and 'Emmerdale'. She asked if I fancied going and I replied that that would be nice, as it turned out to be. On the way there, we stopped in Sheffield and visited a large shopping mall called Meadow Hall. It was whilst walking around this Mall that I saw a very fine bronze statue of three steel workers, which illustrated them pouring molten steel. On returning home I could not get this statue out of my head, for it had woken up an idea, which was that our Docks were at one time the biggest inland docks in the world and there was nothing other than a few elderly cranes to remind anyone of its glorious history. Maybe it was time to put that right, and it was up to me to start the ball rolling.

Now one of my neighbours in Murray Square was a lovely guy called Wally Taylor. He was also a very good artist. One day, I called him over to my home and told him about my idea for a memorial to the history of the Docks. I asked him if he thought he could make a plaster model of a statue if I gave him a basic design of what I had in mind. My outline was that it would be three men standing round a cargo on a wooden pallet. There would be one man standing behind a large sack barrow, a second one standing with a pen and note pad checking the load, and finally, one unhooking the chain which held the cargo in place. Wally made a few sketches until we greed on one that was suitable.

About a week later he presented me with the finished article. I was very impressed, and it was exactly what I wanted. At the next meeting of the Canning Town Partnership, I told them about my idea, and then showed them Wally's work of art. It's fair to say I was pushing on an open door, because they loved both the idea and the model. But most of them knew little or less about bronze statues, so what was decided was that a trip, by the Committee should be made to Sheffield to see if they would be as inspired as I had been: I am pleased to say they were. So they decided to back the idea and to help as much as they could. I had a rough idea of how much the statue would cost because the final sum for completion of the one in Sheffield, was a quarter of a million pounds. However, that statue was life size and the one I had in mind was for each figure to be nine feet tall. So, I had the design, size and material and all I needed now was the site, the money and the artist, easy enough you would have thought. In my dreams!

Another wonderful organisation, of which I was also a member was the Royal Docks Trust. The team there included some really high flyers, and the chair was Eric Sorensen, previously the Head of the London Docklands Development Corporation. His deputy was Richard Gooding, then Chief Executive of the London City Airport: among the other members were lead councillors from Newham. Collectively, they were responsible for many fine projects carried out in the Dockland areas. When I approached them regarding the statue, they readily agreed to manage all of the administration that would be involved, which was a great relief to me because it turned out to be quite arduous. Richard Gooding, via London City Airport, was one of the first contributors, followed closely by the Transport and General Workers Union, and then the Silver Town Development. The Newham Recorder newspaper, was also a great help in the cause, and its participation led to local people donating as individuals.

Another person on the committee was a local Councillor named Patricia Holland. Pat turned out to be a very valuable member in respect of fundraising. I made contact with Ian Shearer who was then, the then Chief Executive of the Excel Exhibition Centre regarding a donation, but Pat had made an inroad already in that direction via Council business. So, when the boss of ExCel agreed to a meeting, Pat was also in attendance. At the meeting I showed Ian Wally's model of the statue, and he said in a strong Scottish accent: "Aye I like that. How much will the statue cost?" I replied that it would be about two hundred and fifty thousand pounds. His reply was: "I dinna like it that much! But I will give you a donation." This turned out to be a very generous one. He also asked how we would like the statue positioned, and indicated that it would be acceptable to be close to the ExCel building. "I would be extremely happy about that" I replied. This would be beneficial in that it would be viewed by thousands of people and at the same time it would be in a secure place: after all, bronze is a valuable metal. During our conversation, Ian asked if we had an artist, to which I replied that we hadn't at the moment. He remarked that one of his friends worked in bronze and that some of her work could be seen in the grounds of the London Zoo and he gave me her details. Then I made contact with she is Wendy Taylor, CBE, was very helpful, but explained that she did not do figurative work. However, she knew someone who did, and this turned out to be an Australian artist named Les Johnson, who in my opinion, is the finest artist for this kind of work, in the world.

Out of interest I found out where Wendy's art work was and went and had a look. One piece, which is the 'Time Piece' is on the Thames embankment next to Tower Bridge, and the other bronze is the 'Dung Beetle' in London's Regent's Park Zoo. Both are totally brilliant pieces of work.

I made contact with Les and a meeting was held at my home. He brought with him some photos of his work, which included a statue of two firemen standing on rubble, fighting a fire with a hose pipe. What struck me the most about this picture, was that one of the fireman had a 'nineteen forties face'. I knew straight away that he was the man for the job. I showed him Wally's model, explained the measurements I had in mind and then we got talking about the cost. He asked me how much I estimated this kind of statue would cost. I already knew the cost of the one in Sheffield, so I went in a bit lower and suggested a hundred and eighty thousand pounds. He gave a wry smile because he too knew the cost of the Sheffield work He said: "Johnny, I think that's a little low, especially taking into consideration the size of each figure that you want". I replied: "Would the fact that the statue site would be almost at the entrance of the Excel building, have any bearing on your thoughts about costs, taking into consideration the amount of exposure to the public it would receive?" Then he came up with a very reasonable quote, leaving us with the problem of how to raise that sum.

In due course I had a meeting with Sir Robin Wales, the Mayor of Newham and he agreed to donate, but it was with a condition. This was that whatever we received in donations within a given time, which he set, the Council would double. Within the allocated time, we received forty seven thousand pounds, which the Council via Sir Robin, increased as he had agreed. On the unveiling day Sir Robin said that he was totally taken aback when he got the news regarding the sum raised, because he didn't think we would be so successful in our aim. Another donation received was from her Majesty the Queen Mother. This was after I had written to her at Clarence house. I informed her of why I thought the Royal docks must not fade into history without something to remind future generations of their glorious past, and then outlined the basic design of the statue. Also, I reminded her Majesty of her visit to Custom House with his Majesty the King, which was just after the Palace had been bombed, and the words she had said then, which were "Now I can face the East End." Although we were told not to disclose the sum donated, we were allowed to say that Her Majesty thought the statue was a wonderful idea, and had made a donation. This fact once published opened a number of doors, which previously might have been a bit stiff to unlock.

The problem with naming people and associations who donated, is that some may be left of the list unintentionally. Suffice it to say that the donors know who they are, so when looking at the statue, be proud because without you, it would not be there.

It was nine long years before my idea became a reality, and all of us who had taken part, assembled for the unveiling. It was a beautiful day for everyone concerned. Among those present was a group of very elderly dockworkers, who like me felt their eyes moisten a number of times. Les Johnson, the artist, put the names of Patricia Holland, Wally Taylor, Mark Tibbs and yours truly on the sides of the cargo crates that are positioned in the middle of the art work, a gesture that was so appreciated by all of us. The figures depicted on the statue are Patrick Holland, a former tally clerk, standing looking at the statue with a pen and notebook in hand; the old fella behind the sack barrow is me, and the young fella with the D.A. haircut is a former professional boxer named Mark Tibbs, a member of the well-known docklands and boxing family. The statue, in all its glory can be seen on the steps that lead from the Dock to the entrance doors of the ExCeL Exhibition Centre, Royal Victoria Dock, Custom House, London E16.

Forty-Three:
On the Move Again 2002

By now, my three sons with their families, had moved away from our area, and one day Brenda said: "John I would like to move nearer the boys." Now, I was not at all sure about this. I loved our little house and had many good friends amongst our neighbours. But since the closure of the docks the area was in serious decline. It seems that now the only thing Custom House is famous for is that it is the rail station for the ExCel Exhibition Centre. I had tried to do what I could to improve the area, by being a member of the Tenants' Association, and the other groups mentioned, and contrary to the views of many local people, I had spoken at a Public Enquiry in favour of the now firmly established London City Airport, when my thinking had been that we required something to kick start the regeneration of the area. So, my investment in the area was considerable.

I answered Brenda as follows: "I am not sure about moving mate, but I will pray about it". Unlike me, my wife is not a Christian, but if my prayers are answered she will be one day. So I went upstairs, knelt down and said this prayer. Lord my wife has asked me to move home to be nearer our sons. I am seeking your guidance, and the answer I got back was a very clear "I WIIL BLESS THAT". Now, I really was not expecting that, so I asked: "But Lord, what about all the work you have given me to do in this area?" Again came the reply: "I WILL BLESS THE MOVE". So I went downstairs and said: "All right darling, we are moving."

Came the day of the move in June 2002, into the moving van went all our belongings, and after thirty two years in a very happy home, I closed the front door of our lovely little house for the last time. I bid a fond farewell to our neighbours and off we went to a lovely little bungalow in Harold Park near Romford, Essex. It took well over six months and a good deal of money before Brenda and I agreed that we have now put the Ringwood stamp on it. Next thing to sort out was the garden. This was quite a task. I should have realised that when we viewed it prior to buying, I noticed two pair of wellingtons on the conservatory steps. Soon after moving in there was a very heavy thunderstorm, and in a very short time our garden had become a lake, the reason being that there were only a few inches of earth and underneath this was about eight feet of good old Essex clay. So, being a keen gardener I listened to the experts, hired a small digger, with which I dug a trench all the way along the perimeter fence to a depth of five feet, and in the bottom of which I laid a large perforated soakaway pipe. On the top of that I laid seven tons of pebbles, which should have done the job. It didn't. As soon as we had another heavy downpour, back came the lake. To overcome the problem, I found out where the lowest part of the garden was and dug a deep hole into which I put a very large plastic drum, having drilled the sides of it with hundreds of holes. Then I surrounded the drum with fine gravel to act as a filter, and finally fitted a submersible pump, and connected the whole thing to the main drain and electrics. Hey presto! A well-drained garden was the end product of all this labour.

Harold Park is a lovely little area, and once again we are blessed with wonderful neighbours who made us very welcome as soon as we arrived. I now worship in a little church in Harold Hill called St Pauls, and once again I have found true fellowship. Harold Hill has a large council estate which was built just after the Second World War, and many of the original tenants came from the East End of London. It still retains much of the culture from that area, so I knew that the St Pauls congregation were my kind of people and felt at home immediately.

Also, I was blessed with a good vicar whose name is Russel Moul. His preaching is very direct and to the point, with little or no room for compromise and his main thrust is that if that is what the Bible states, then that is what will be reflected in his sermons. This stance has put him at loggerheads with the more liberal branches of the clergy on a number of occasions.

Not only is he good from the front of the church, but along with his wife Alie, has reached out into the local community and given very tangible support in many areas.

Forty-Four:
The Steam Ship Robin

I return to Canning Town about every six weeks to visit the Peacock Gym, both to meet up with old mates and to have a couple of hours' training session. Also, I always make a trip to the Victoria dock to keep an eye on the statue. It was during one of these occasions that I viewed the SS Robin on the other side of the dock sitting on the top of a floating pontoon. Previously I had known her when I was working for the security company, but at that time she had been moored in the West India Quay. I went over to her position and found that there was a site office that dealt with visitors to the boat, so I went in and asked if there was any chance of going on board. When I explained about my time as a Merchant Seamen, they knew that my interest had some foundation other than that of a tourist. Without going into much depth with regards to the 'Robin's' history, suffice it to say that she was built in 1890 and was the first of her type. Further details can be found on the SS Robin web page. The main thrust of her future is to make the boat much more than a tourist attraction, and to provide more educational value. But because of her age and general state of repair, a great deal of money is required to achieve this aim. I asked if I could I could be of help in any way and the guy in charge said that filmed interviews were going to take place in the very near future, regarding fund raising. He asked if I would like to take part because of my naval and local area background. This I readily agreed to. It had some success but not enough, which is very sad, because in my opinion the Robin is equally as important in Maritime History as the Cutty Sark. She is the only one in existence of her type in the world.

After interviewing a group of interested parties including myself, the fella who was carrying out the filming asked me if I could do one on my own. "About what?" I enquired. He replied: "Just talk about yourself as a local dockland's man." The end product can now be seen on YouTube entitled 'Johnny Ringwood interview 2014'.

Following that, I joined a group of local dockland folk who were being interviewed for a project called Forgotten Stories. The outcome of this can be viewed, by visiting the web site "Forgotten Stories Royal Dock." On the day of the launch of the above, I was requested to attend, which of course, I accepted. Then I received an Email asking me to attend before 9am. The reason for this was that I was to be interviewed on live television, which seemed to go down well enough. Then a couple of hours later I was again approached by the organisers who said: "Johnny you are on again, but this time it's BBC1. Are you OK with that?" "Not a problem" I replied. The delightful young lady from the BBC1 programme who was to carry out the interview was Ayshea Buksh. We had a brief talk prior to the filming, about my input on the project, and during this conversation the Dockers' Statue was mentioned. Her reaction was to say: "That sounds like a wonderful place to carry out the interview." So, it went ahead as planned and because it was not live, I had time to telephone my wife Brenda who notified all and sundry, that the old man was going to get his fifteen minutes of fame, which was about the length of the actual interview. However, when it finally went out it was condensed to about two minutes, but it was long enough to get my picture in the frame, this time for something very worthwhile.

Forty-Five:
Finally

Our family has grown and our three sons have given us seven wonderful grandchildren. They are: Billy, Georgia, Danielle, John, Nicky, Isobelle and Michael, and as an added bonus our eldest grandson Billy and his lovely lady Jodie have just presented Brenda and I with our first Great Grandchild who has been named Frankie.

My initial introduction to gardening at the Fyfield (fattening up) School has stood me in good stead. My garden recently received "A Garden of Excellence Certificate" from a competition run by Havering Council. Some of my best times are now spent during a summer's evening, sitting on my swing seat in the far corner of this garden, listening to good jazz coming from my award winning shed, which was voted Daily Mirror Shed of the year, 2014. Set alongside me on the adjoining table is a bowl of fresh cockles, and potato crisps, but the lemonade that was enjoyed so long ago in the foyer of the Peacock pub, has now been replaced with a cold glass of very good Chablis.

I have recently celebrated my eighty-first birthday and I can honestly say that I have been blessed in so many ways. Yes of course there have been ups and downs, but that's the tapestry of life.

So I will close, hoping you have enjoyed the memoirs of a now very content, elderly man.

"God Bless"

Printed in Great Britain
by Amazon